THE MASONIC/ CHRISTIAN CONFLICT EXPLAINED

All Scripture quotations in this book are taken from the King James translation of the Bible.

The Masonic/Christian Conflict Explained

Copyright © 2005 by Keith Harris
Original copyright 1993
P.O. Box 1353 Madisonville, KY 42431
www.scripture2scripture.com
Published by The Olive Press
An Olive Press Production

Copy Typist: Lynn Jeffcoat
Copy Editor: Susanna Cancassi
Proofreaders: Angie Peters, Susanna Cancassi
Layout/Design: Michelle Kim
Lithography: Simon Froese
Cover Design: Michelle Kim

Library of Congress Cataloging-in-Publication Data

Harris, Keith
    The Masonic/Christian Conflict Explained
    ISBN# 0-937422-61-4

    1. Freemasonry   2. Apologetics   3. Criticism/ Interpretation

I am honored to see this book catapult into its fourth printing, especially with its new facelift and expansion. I have great expectations for this latest printing because of the positive responses and testimonies I've received about lives that have already been changed. Due to an overwhelming interest in the subject and the desire of many to know more, I have been privileged to update and expand its content. This has been my prayer from the very start. Prayerfully consider reaching your Masonic friends with the documented facts that expose the conflict between Christian and Masonic principles.

May God bless you as you continue to seek His face.

I would like to express my gratitude to Arno Froese, Susanna Cancassi, Angie Peters and Michelle Kim of Midnight Call Ministries for their support and labor on this project. I would also like to thank my wife, Cindy, for her wonderful support through the long hours put into the research and commitment that went into the production of this book.

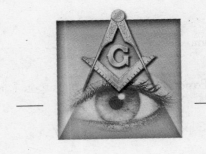

CONTENTS

Introduction 9

A Past Master's Testimony 13

Chapter 1: Masonic Teachings vs. Christian Principles . . .15

Chapter 2: Good Works and the Bible 29

Chapter 3: Sons of Light 37

Chapter 4: Oaths: Binding Sanctions 45

Chapter 5: Masonic Roots: Christ, Solomon or Baal? 55

Chapter 6: Freemasonry and the Luciferian Connection . .75

Chapter 7: Freemasonry and Islam 85

Chapter 8: The Eastern Star: Binding the Masonic Family . .95

Chapter 9: The Superiority of Freemasonry 105

Chapter 10: Come Now, Let Us Reason Together 117

Appendix

   A. Kabbala 129

   B. Spurious Freemasonry 135

   C. The Trinity of Baalim 141

   D. Freemasonry and the New Age Revival 147

Glossary of Masonic Terms 153

Bibliography 161

Index 165

INTRODUCTION

A growing interest in the Christian community revolves around memberships in organizations outside of the church. Christian involvement in one organization in particular is especially disturbing. Whether you are considering becoming involved in the Masonic Lodge, are a long-time Lodge member, or are a church member who has friends in the Lodge, you owe it to yourself to become informed about this important issue.

The beliefs and teachings of Masonry are surfacing to reveal doctrine that separates Freemasonry from Christianity. These revelations put to rest one of the most common beliefs among Masons: that Freemasonry is a Christian organization.

The perception that Masonry is indeed a Christian organization springs in part from the fact that many ministers and laymen are climbing the Masonic ranks. The Lodge boasts a roster full of Christians, and while its affiliation with the church is not the foremost enticement for men to join the Lodge, it is without doubt a principal attraction, especially among other church members who may also be considering joining. Such persuasion, among other things, has brought recognition to the Order as being the world's largest fraternal organization.

Freemasonry is an international fraternity based on "morality veiled in allegory and illustrated by symbols" (*Freemasonry*, Martin L. Wagner, pg. 38). The practices of withholding secrets from outsiders and members of inferior degree earn the organization the title of "secret society" even though Freemasonry is not a hidden organization.

Masonic literature relates, "The history of Masonry is the history of philosophy" (*Morals and Dogma*, pg. 504). This "speculative inquiry concerning the source and nature of human knowledge" is taught degree by degree through rituals and oaths, which involve the candidate's endless search for "light."

The word "free" added to the word "Masonry" distinguishes between "operative" and "speculative" Masonry. Under the heading "Free" in the *Encyclopedia of Freemasonry*, written by Albert Mackey and Charles T. McClenachan, both 33rd–degree Masons, we learn that in connection with the word "Mason," the word "free" originally meant that the person so called was free of the company or gild of incorporated Masons.

With the exception of progressive alterations, Freemasonry is identical to the ancient mystery religions (*Morals and Dogma*, pg. 624), especially those of ancient Egypt. Although the era of Solomon's temple plays an integral role in Masonic lore, much of the symbolisms, appellations, and rituals stem from Egyptian legend. Freemasonry preserves the traditional practices of Old Testament Baal worship, which will be reviewed in Chapter Five.

Although it is wholly uncongenial for a member of the Order to persuade anyone to join, many take it upon themselves to urge their friends or relatives to do so. Chances are, you too may have been directly or indirectly encouraged to become a member.

This book is not such a solicitation. It is a source of information designed to compare Masonic and biblical doctrine. If the Masonic/Christian conflict is to be reviewed correctly, then evidence from authoritative Masonic figures must be used rather than information from local Lodge members or sincere individuals sold on the "rightness" of the Lodge.

Although the works of several Masonic writers will be cited in this study, in no way do I intend to tarnish or malign their personal character or the character of other Lodge members.

Thomas Jefferson said, "Men are inherently capable of making proper judgments when they are properly informed" (*The Art of Speaking*, Elson, Peck). Thus the purpose of this book: to inform the reader about both sides of the ever-growing Masonic/Christian conflict.

–Keith Harris

A Past Master's Testimony

I know how easy it is to defend the Lodge and how hard it is to accept Christian scrutiny of Masonry. For I was in the Lodge for 14 years, reaching the 32nd–degree level, and was Master of the Lodge for six years. For most of those years I too defended and justified my membership in the Lodge and discounted all Christian "attacks" against it.

However, being a seeker of truth and light, as you are, the more I searched the more I found Masonry to conflict with and oppose the teachings of Jesus Christ. The two could not be yoked together. I had to divest myself of Freemasonry. I would strongly urge all Masons to sincerely evaluate in whose light they stand, and in whom do they put their trust.

–Rev. Kurt Leberman, former 32rd–degree
Mason and past Master

CHAPTER
1

MASONIC TEACHING VS. CHRISTIAN PRINCIPLES

Freemasonry has been credited with making good men better. In other words, it is said to miraculously transform inherently sinful traits into positive characteristics such as hope, love and charity. Masonic teaching emphasizes morality and virtue in the social stratum. Since it is presumed that "good" men produce "good" behavior, such men seek to associate with certain benevolent societies that will express their desire of virtue in a larger realm. For many, Freemasonry fulfills that "moral" need.

...a great number of Masons belong to and even govern many church bodies.

I have found personally that, among the Masons who profess to be Christians, morality and integrity greatly influence their allegiance to the Lodge. Although they enjoy other membership benefits such as business acquaintances, friendships, and other material advantages, morality and good works stand out as the chief reasons men enjoy being Masons. It is common knowledge that one must possess a certain amount of good character in order to be granted Lodge membership.

On the other hand, there is a growing interest in the organization among Christians who wonder whether Lodge principles are truly God's principles. This line of questioning stems from the display of a Bible on Lodge altars and the prayers offered to God from behind closed Lodge doors. This has become a major cause for concern because a great number of Masons belong to and even govern many church bodies.

In order to present both sides of the issue, we must consider some basic questions: Is Freemasonry a religion? If so, is it Christian? Does Lodge practice recognize Jesus as Lord and God's only begotten Son? What authority does the Bible have in the Lodge? Does Freemasonry offer a plan of salvation? Is the Lodge just another club?

Is Freemasonry a Religion?

The mention of the words "Mason" and "religion" in the same sentence immediately spark heated debates among a number of devout Masons. Many Christians also express a strong distaste when Christianity is referred to as a "religion." So what constitutes a religion, and does Freemasonry merit placement in that category?

Although any group that presents itself as being "true" or possessing the "truth" dislikes being classified as a "religion," we must understand that any group or institution should logically be considered a religion if it meets many or all of the following criteria: meets on a regular basis, uses altars, prays to a deity, holds rituals, baptizes, meets in temples, has deacons, serves communion, and operates according to a generally-agreed-upon doctrine. With this in mind, we can consider several authoritative Masonic writings.

In his book *Morals and Dogma* (Masonic doctrine and usage for superior degrees), Albert Pike, a 33rd–degree Mason and Grand Commander to the Supreme Council for the 33rd–degree of Freemasonry, wrote: "Every Masonic temple is a temple of religion." And under the heading "Religion of Freemasonry," we read this explanation by Mackey and McClenachan, in the *Encyclopedia of Freemasonry* (pg. 213):

> The tendency of all true Masonry is toward religion. If it make any progress, its progress is to that holy end. Look at its ancient landmarks, its sublime ceremonies, its profound symbols and allegories — all religious doctrine, inculcating [commanding] religious observance, and teaching religious truth, and who can deny that it is eminently a religious institution?

So, according to its own authorities, Freemasonry is, by practice and definition, indeed a religion.

We also find outstanding reverence in the organization. On page 6 of the book *What is Freemasonry?* (issued by the Grand Lodge of Illinois, 1965), we read: "The first and most important belief of Freemasonry is a belief in God. There is no secular test as each member is free to select his own religious principle."

The membership requirement of having a belief in God is good in and of itself; however, we must remember that "principles" (the guidelines or rules of conduct) are what make us Christian, Buddhist, Muslim, etc. Contrary to increasingly popular belief, all religions are not Christian.

Is Freemasonry Christian?

Under the heading, "Christianization of Freemasonry," in the *Encyclopedia of Freemasonry*, we read: "If Masonry were simply a Christian institution, the Jew and the Muslim, the Brahman and the Buddhist could not conscientiously partake of its illumination. But its universality is its boast" (pg. 148).

So we see that Freemasonry is not "simply" Christian. In other words, Freemasonry is more than, or superior to, if it is "not simply."

This boast of universality or the allowance of each member's religious preference means members cannot recognize Jesus as "the" redeemer because that would offend a Buddhist. Neither can the Lodge recognize Buddha as being "the" sole redeemer because that would offend a Christian. Such a universal, non-sectarian creed is one of Freemasonry's great boasts.

In order to maintain a "religious" balance, especially in large city Lodges, general names for God must be used. Some of those names include: Grand Architect; Great Architect of the Universe; Supreme Being; Master; Grand Warden of Heaven; and Legislator. A sectarian allows Jesus' name to be used for Buddha in prayers or similar observances.

We find this sentiment recorded under Article II, section III in the *By-Laws of the M.W. Grand Lodge of Illinois* (relating to disciplinary proceedings). Notice the words "specifications" and "sectarian

19

character" in this quote: "The Master of any lodge shall not permit any charges or specifications, or any other subject matter, either written or oral, involving questions of a political or sectarian character, to be read in, or in any manner presented to, the Lodge."

"But My Lodge Recognizes Jesus"

Although rural Lodges may use Jesus' name in a prayer or refer to Him as "Lord," this practice is against the rules of the Grand Lodge. In fact, members are sworn under oath to report such distinct referrals to a redeemer.

In Colossians 3:17, the Apostle Paul wrote: "Whatsoever ye do in word or deed, do all in the name of the Lord Jesus, giving thanks to God and the Father by him."

How then does Freemasonry acknowledge Jesus?

A regular or well-governed Masonic Lodge does not permit its members to pray in the name of Jesus; thus, the Mason who does recognize Jesus in the Lodge as "the" Redeemer is not being true to Masonry. Likewise, the Mason who claims to be a Christian yet who does not recognize Jesus in the Lodge or pray in His name is not being true to Christianity. This is a no-win situation!

How then does Freemasonry acknowledge Jesus? Albert Pike wrote the following in his book, *Morals and Dogma:*

Masonry, around whose altars the Christian, the

Hebrew, the [Muslim], the Brahmin, the followers of Confucius and Zoroaster, can assemble as brethren and unite in prayer to the one God who is above all the Baalim, must needs to leave it to each of its initiates to look for the foundation of his faith and hope to the written scriptures of his own religion (pg. 226).

We have seen that Freemasonry recognizes no particular redeemer, yet places an emphasis on God. Here, we find prayers offered "to the one God who is above all the Baalim." This type of universality places Christ Jesus in the category of all the Baalim! The word "Baalim" denotes a false god or idol. Little wonder the conflict continues to grow!

Christian Principle

Regardless of an individual's personal convictions as to the identity of Jesus Christ, his membership in any group, organization, or club that degrades the deity of Christ places him in grave danger.

An organization, regardless of its type, should not be considered Christian on the basis of having members on the roll who profess Christianity. Nor can claims of brotherhood, equality, liberty, or even good works justify labeling someone as a Christian. The only way for a person to be correctly identified as a Christian is for him or her to believe in no one but Jesus Christ as the only means of salvation and for that person to maintain a lifestyle that reflects such a claim.

The word "Christ" is used to reveal that He is the

Anointed, the Messiah and God incarnate. John 3:16 says Jesus is the only begotten Son. Hebrews 1:3 says Jesus is the "express image of his person" (i.e., the exact portrait of God in essence and in self).

To demote Christ Jesus to any position other than God in the flesh is to label one's self as antichrist.

Jesus' deity is also realized in the name "Emmanuel," which is interpreted as "God with us" (Matthew 1:23). Even the name "Jesus" (*Iesous*, Greek) comes from the Hebrew name "Jehoshua" (*Yehowshuwa*), which means "Jehovah is salvation."

For comparison, we refer to Isaiah 43:11, in which Jehovah God said, "I, even I, am the LORD; and beside me there is no saviour." In Luke 2:11, the angel of the Lord, speaking of Jesus, proclaimed: "For unto you is born this day in the city of David a Saviour, which is Christ the LORD." To demote Christ Jesus to any position other than God in the flesh (John 1:1,14) is to label one's self as antichrist. "For many deceivers are entered into the world, who confess not that Jesus Christ is come in the flesh. This is a deceiver and an antichrist" (2 John 7).

Like other religions, Freemasonry is sure to recognize Jesus as existing in the flesh but fails to stress the appellative office or epithet of Christ. Many good men have been deceived into accepting only the mention of Jesus as redeemer and have been hoodwinked to the degradation of the person of Jesus. This degradation is found in identifying Jesus as a mere reformer, as revealed by Masonic writers:

In *Morals and Dogma*, Pike wrote:

> [Masonry] reverences all the great reformers. It sees in Moses, the Lawgiver of the Jews, in Confucius and Zoroaster, in Jesus of Nazareth, and in the Arabian Iconoclast [Mohammed], great teachers of morality and eminent reformers, if no more: and allows every brother of the Order to assign to each such higher and even divine character as his creed and truth require (pg. 525).

This would say to the Christian: "Jesus was a great teacher of morality and an eminent reformer, if no more. You may assign to Him divine character, if you desire, but we [Freemasonry] do not."

The Bible teaches that to deny Jesus is not to deny His existence but to deny His authority. First John 2:23 says: "Whosoever denieth the Son [Jesus as the Christ], the same hath not the Father."

Deceived?

It becomes evident that those who believe Freemasonry is compatible with Christianity are being deceived, for there are those in the Lodge who would not knowingly participate in anything that would degrade Christ. Not only does it appear to be deception but we find it to be a fact, according to Pike.

> The Blue Degrees are but the outer court or portico

23

of the Temple. Part of the symbols are displayed there to the initiate, but he is intentionally misled by false interpretations. It is not intended that he shall understand them; but it is intended that he shall imagine he understands them (*Morals and Dogma,* pg. 819).

Many Masons refer to the "Blue Degrees" (first three) as the "Christian" degrees. According to the above, this is a blatant lie that has cunningly trickled down to inferior-degree members who have been mentally conditioned to believe and accept it as the truth. (And this is called integrity?) These false interpretations appear to be truthful to a lower-degreed member, making them nearly impossible to reach with biblical principles that contradict Freemasonry.

Philosophy Principle

Since Freemasonry requires one to believe in God, yet it endorses no particular redeemer, the Order must present itself as possessing complete truth concerning God's principles.

In *Encyclopedia of Freemasonry,* under the heading "Christianization of Freemasonry," we read:

> It is true that it embraces within its scheme the great truths of Christianity, upon the subject of the immortality of the soul and the resurrection of the body; but this was to be presumed, because Freemasonry is truth, and all truth must be identical. But the origin of each is different; their histories are dissimilar (pg. 148).

24

If Freemasonry is true and its history is dissimilar to Christianity, then Christianity must only be an abstract or an incomplete version of the truth, especially its claim that Jesus is the Way, the Truth, and the Life. Since all truth must be identical, it should now be clear that a drastic conflict exists between Masonic teachings and biblical principles.

Another Way?

To contain such conflicting elements, yet believe in the immortality of the soul and the resurrection of the body, it becomes clear that an avenue for such beliefs in Lodge teachings must be found. This avenue is symbolized by the raising of the candidate from death to life in the Third-Degree ritual (Master Mason Degree).

Following preliminary ritual, the candidate lays down on the floor, symbolizing the death of Hiram, a man from Tyre and a widow's son who was killed while he worked on King Solomon's temple. After futile attempts by the senior and junior wardens to raise the candidate, the Master of the Lodge uses the "Strong Grip" or "Lion's Paw Grip," which represents King Solomon, to successfully raise the candidate to new life.

The following information is listed in the *Encyclopedia of Freemasonry*, under the heading "Raised":

When a candidate has received the Third Degree, he is said to have been "raised" to the sublime degree of a Master Mason. The expression refers, materially, to a portion of the ceremony of initiation, but symbolically, to the resurrection, which it is the object of the degree to exemplify (pg. 607).

When a candidate has received the Third Degree, he is said to have been "raised" to the sublime degree of a Master Mason.

A further explanation of the condition of this "raised" person is given under the heading "regeneration." This person is supposedly raised into a philosophy of regeneration, or the new birth of all things. This philosophy is a speculation of regeneration. Although many who have professed Christianity recognize the difference between this ritual and Christian practice, and brush it off as being merely symbolic, many accept this ritual as being the actual regeneration or new birth. They believe this will get them to the "Grand Lodge above." To confirm this, ask a Mason who is not affiliated with a church. He will probably assure you, "The Lodge is good enough for me."

In the Bible such a philosophy or symbolic search is called a "form," which comes from the Greek word *morphosis*, meaning "formation or fashion, implying appearance or semblance, which is a representation, or something that symbolizes."

This "form" of godliness is deceptive and is apparently the reason that seldom does one reach the unchurched Mason with the biblical truth of new birth: salvation. (Deception appears to be much like the truth, even in theory, so that many perceive it to actually be truth.)

Merriam-Webster defines the word "philosophy" as being "a speculative inquiry concerning the source and nature of human knowledge or a system of ideas based on such thinking." The art of philosophy in terms of religion is to extract only those common characteristics from each religion to form a perspective of their perception of truth. Such is the universality of Freemasonry.

Albert Pike confirms, "The history of Masonry is the history of Philosophy" (*Morals and Dogma,* pg. 540). And again he relates, "Philosophy is a kind of journey, ever learning yet never arriving at the ideal perfection of truth" (*Morals and Dogma*, pg. 691).

This statement should sound familiar to Christians, for it was under the inspiration and the authority of the Holy Spirit that the Apostle Paul warned Timothy about those who would possess a "form" of godliness, but would deny the power thereof (2 Timothy 3:5).

The Apostle related that such people are: "Ever learning, and never able to come to the knowledge of the truth" (2 Timothy 3:7).

And to the Colossians he wrote: "Beware lest any man spoil you through philosophy and vain deceit, after the tradition of men, after the rudiments of the world, and not after Christ. For in him dwelleth all the fullness of the Godhead [divinity-Greek] bodily" (Colossians 2:8–9).

CHAPTER
2

GOOD WORKS AND
THE BIBLE

Perhaps no aspect of the Masonic philosophy is as popular or as widely known or admired as that of its good works. Numerous reports document the clinics, hospitals, nursing homes and individuals who have been assisted by the Lodge. This is indeed admirable but we mustn't allow ourselves to be swept away by the "rightness" of what the Masons are doing and lose sight of their inescapable wrongs when their philosophy is compared to biblical Christian principles.

Good works do not merit any eternal value beyond the realm of human existence.

The Apostle Paul explained: "Not by works of righteousness which we have done, but according to his mercy he saved us, by the washing of regeneration, and renewing of the Holy Ghost" (Titus 3:5).

Good works do not merit any eternal value beyond the realm of human existence. Only after a person has accepted Jesus Christ as Lord are his works deposited into an eternal account. Addressing believers, Paul wrote: "For we must all appear before the judgment seat of Christ; that every one may receive the things done in his body, according to that he hath done, whether it be good or bad" (2 Corinthians 5:10).

Yet Freemasonry places good works on an eternal pedestal:

> There is perennial [everlasting] nobleness and even sacredness in work. Be he never so benighted and for-

getful of his high calling, there is always hope in a
man who actually and earnestly works: In idleness
alone is there perpetual despair. Man perfects himself
by working (*Morals and Dogma*, pgs. 341–342).

The problem lies in the system of "salvation by
works" when you realize the "new birth" offered by
Lodge rituals is only symbolic, while good works are
literal.

Consider this excerpt taken from the words spoken
at a Masonic funeral: "This Mason was true to all
our teachings, and the apron he now wears in the cas-
ket represents that purity of life and conduct by
which he will now gain admission into the Celestial
Lodge above."

Clearly revealed in this quote is Masonry teaches
that its followers will enter heaven by following
Lodge doctrine and by living pure lives or by doing
good works. Does Masonry transform a good man
into a better man according to biblical standards?
No. A person is saved only by grace through faith in
Jesus Christ!

Ephesians 2:8–10 says: "For by grace are ye saved
through faith; and that not of yourselves: it is the gift
of God: Not of works, lest any man should boast.
For we are his workmanship, created in Christ Jesus
unto good works, which God hath before ordained
that we should walk in them."

That Lodge members carry out good works cannot
be denied, nor can it be said that Masonic teaching is

completely wrong. According to biblical principles, however, Masonic truths are not complete, nor are they absolute. They are nothing short of deceptive. Although the good works are to be admired, nothing is so deceptive, especially to those who have had only a pale representation of the new birth, that is, "a representation of a regeneration."

Biblical Principles

Scripture is certainly sprinkled throughout Masonic literature. Familiar Bible verses permeate Masonic teaching, especially those surrounding the Solomon era.

Why does Lodge teaching refer to the Bible?

As we see Masonic doctrine continue to contradict the Bible, we must ask: Why does Lodge teaching refer to the Bible? Is it for the truth it contains or is there another reason?

Pike wrote this about the Bible:

> The Bible is an indispensable part of the furniture of a Christian Lodge, only because it is the sacred book of the Christian religion. The Hebrew Pentateuch in a Hebrew Lodge, and the Koran in the Mohammedan one, belong on the altar; and one of these, and the square and compass, properly understood, are the great lights by which a Mason must walk (*Morals and Dogma,* pg. 11).

In the *Encyclopedia of Freemasonry,* Mackey and

McClenachan adds this insight:

> The Bible is used among Masons as a symbol of the will of God, however, it may be expressed. And, therefore, whatever to any people expressed that will may be used as a substitute for the Bible in a Masonic Lodge.

This quote reveals that the Bible is not displayed in the Lodge because it contains the truth but, as Pike puts it, because it is considered nothing more than part of the decor. This point is further exemplified by the Lodge's demonstration of political correctness in displaying other religious writings on its altars. According to Masonic teaching, the Bible is incomplete and is only a part of God's overall truth.

Christians believe the Bible alone is God's complete counsel to man; it is not a mere symbol or a piece of furniture! A symbol is only a representation of something that is real. Thus, Masonic philosophy has placed God's Word on the same level as many religious writings that reject Jesus Christ.

Although Lodge teachings apply many Scripture verses to "Masonic principle," only passages that are used in a universal sense have been borrowed. Additionally, as a non-sectarian Order, certain verses used by natural course must omit phrases that mention Jesus by name (in a regular or well-governed Lodge). Most Masons are unaware of this practice of omission, which Mackey calls "a slight but necessary modification" (*Masonic Ritualist*, pg. 272).

For example, 2 Thessalonians 3:6 says: "Now we command you, brethren, *in the name of our Lord Jesus Christ*, that ye withdraw yourselves from every brother that walketh disorderly, and not after the tradition which he received of us." The italicized portion of that verse is not used in the Lodge (see also 1 Peter 2:5).

It becomes clear that having a holy book on its altars, regardless of the religion it represents, serves one purpose: To fulfill the requirement that a sacred article must be present to swear in new candidates. This is done so that it appears to the initiate, Christian or otherwise, that he is trespassing against his own personal faith if he breaks his Masonic oath.

We are not to be unitarian in a manner that unites us with cults that reject Jesus; we are called to be a separate people.

The truth is that when the doctrinal stance of any group has been stripped away, how a person views the deity of Christ, the plan of salvation, and the Bible are the criteria for labeling that person "Christian" or "anti-Christian."

Masonic authorities classify Jesus as being only a reformer or a high teacher; they teach that salvation is obtainable only by works; and they hold that the Bible is only a portion or an incomplete version of God's overall truth. These are blatant contradictions to Christianity.

On the other hand, the Bible teaches that Jesus is God's only begotten Son (John 3:16). By comparison, Jesus and not the Lodge is the only foundation upon which to build (1 Corinthians 3:11). We are not to be unitarian in a manner that unites us with cults that reject Jesus; we are called to be a separate people.

Second Corinthians 6:17–18 says: "Wherefore come out from among them, and be ye separate, saith the Lord, and touch not the unclean thing; and I will receive you, And will be a Father unto you, and ye shall be my sons and daughters, saith the Lord Almighty."

To strive for a righteous end with unrighteous means only adds measure to the need.

CHAPTER
3

SONS OF LIGHT

We have learned that Masonry classifies Jesus as a reformer or high teacher, and that the Bible is displayed only as a symbol and furthermore is rendered as being incomplete. It must surely be noteworthy that if these assumptions were true, the Order must, in turn, present itself as possessing absolute truth. This thesis is further substantiated by the use of the word "light."

The word "light" is an important term in Freemasonry. According to Mackey, it is "the first of all the symbols presented to the neophyte (initiate) and continues to be presented to him in various modifications throughout all his future progress in his Masonic career" (*Encyclopedia of Freemasonry*, pg. 446).

Light not only makes things visible but also is a symbolic term that generally refers to truth. In Scripture, "light" occasionally refers to man's intellect (Isaiah 50:11) or God's Word (Psalm 119:105). It also describes a Christian who walks with God (Ephesians 5:8) or his testimony (Matthew 5:16). Most importantly, true Light is none other than Jesus Christ; He set the foundation for such a belief (John 8:12). Masons, however, consider themselves as possessors of unadulterated light and refer to themselves as "sons of light."

Under the heading "light," the *Encyclopedia of Freemasonry* relates:

> Freemasons are emphatically called the "sons of light" because they are, or at least are entitled to be, in possession of the true meaning of the symbol; while

the profane or uninitiated who have not received the knowledge are, by a parity of expression, said to be in darkness (pg. 446).

It becomes increasingly clear that Christians and Masons have a very different interpretation of the word "light." A Christian man who comes to the Lodge to be initiated is considered ignorant of the true meaning of the symbol; thus, we refer to the "Apprentice Degree" introduction: Following three distinct knocks on the door the senior deacon asks, "Who comes here?" The junior deacon, speaking on behalf of the initiate, replies: "Rev. James Hunt, who has long been in darkness, and now seeks to be brought to light, and to receive a part in the rights and benefits of this worshipful Lodge, erected to God and dedicated to the Saints John, as all brothers and fellows have done before" (*Ronayne's Handbook of Freemasonry,* pg. 57).

For a Christian to admit he is in darkness would be an admission that the light given him through Christ Jesus is not sufficient or even valid.

John 8:12 says: "Then spake Jesus again unto them, saying, I am the light of the world: he that followeth me shall not walk in darkness, but shall have the light of life." And 1 John 1:5 says, "This then is the message which we have heard of him, and declare unto you, that God is light, and in him is no darkness at all." A shudder of fear would surely enter the Christian's mind at the mere suggestion that he is in darkness and needs to be brought into the light.

Light can also be considered a figure of speech relating to the believer's state after he leaves Satan's kingdom of darkness and enters God's kingdom of light (Acts 26:18). This does not happen through Masonic rituals but by having faith in Jesus Christ (Romans 10:9). Yet, many who profess to be Christians have personally experienced or witnessed the following ritual: Candidates don initiation apparel that leaves their left arm and breast exposed. They are blindfolded (hoodwinked) and have a rope (cable-tow) around their neck. They agree when told they are in darkness that they desire to be brought to the light.

These initiates are therefore referred to as "sons of light," which also makes apparent yet another contradiction. Ephesians 5:13 plainly states in part: "whatsoever doth make manifest is light." Yet these "sons of light" swear oaths to ever conceal and never reveal — and that under the penalty of mutilation and death!

It is puzzling that many ministers, deacons and church members do not realize these conflicts between the principles of the two organizations— that is, until the element of deception is considered. We must keep in mind that a person who is already convinced of the righteousness of any group or organization will be blind to its error; one does not find evil when he does not look for evil. "Christian" ministers and laymen have only added to the deception.

The fact that many ministers are members of the

Lodge attracts otherwise uninterested people into considering Lodge membership. Ministers of the Gospel are to be overseers of God's people. The overseers of God's people in the Old Testament caused national decline because of outside influences provided by groups such as Freemasonry. We see this through the prophet Jeremiah. "Many pastors have destroyed my vineyard, they have trodden my portion under foot, they have made my pleasant portion a desolate wilderness...The spoilers are come upon all high places through the wilderness: for the sword of the LORD shall devour from the one end of the land even to the other end of the land: no flesh shall have peace" (Jeremiah 12:10, 12).

Ministers of the Gospel are to be overseers of God's people.

This happened because the pastors had taught the people to swear by Baal (Jeremiah 12:16) and not to swear that the "Lord liveth."

Note of Interest

Many Bible passages relate that such false worship was commonly held on "high places" or on "high hills." Under the heading "highest hills" in the *Encyclopedia of Freemasonry*, we read: "In the Old York lectures was the following passage: 'Before we had the convenience of such well-formed Lodges, the Brethren used to meet on the highest hills and in the lowest of valleys'" (pg. 325).

During such worship the candidate would kiss the respective idol, revealing his absolute respect and adoration, thus sealing his obligation (1 Kings 19:18; Hosea 13:2).

Following the oath of obligation, the Worshipful Master (Master of the Lodge) instructs: "In token of your sincerity, you will detach your hands and kiss the Bible" (*Ronayne's Handbook of Freemasonry*, pg. 70).

Jeremiah 12:17 contains a plea from the Lord for these pastors to learn the ways of the people and to swear by His name that He lives. He warns: "But if they will not obey, I will utterly pluck up and destroy that nation, saith the LORD."

God's Word will not return to Him void.

Even though personal or community needs might be met through our churches under the direction of a minister who is also a Mason, we must remember that it is God who meets our needs regardless of the means. God's Word will not return to Him void; that is not necessarily true of man.

An example of this is found in chapters 22–25 of the book of Numbers. God used a soothsayer named Balaam to bless Israel. Although God used Balaam to utter correct prophecy, this man was not of God. Balaam's downfall, which led to his death, was his inherent sin. Many Israelites perished with him (Numbers 25:9; 31:8,16).

Although Masons may not personally be wicked or

evil, Freemasonry doctrine is when compared to Christianity. If Christianity is indeed "incomplete," as Masonry relates, then it is of no consequence. If Christianity is true, then these men have been deceived into participating in anti-Christian practices.

Like others, ministers who become Masons readily accept superficial pretense without searching the matter any further; thus, they too become duped by a false light: "And no marvel; for Satan himself is transformed into an angel of light. Therefore it is no great thing if his ministers also be transformed as the ministers of righteousness; whose end shall be according to their works" (2 Corinthians 11:14–15).

In other words, there are ministers who proclaim righteousness but who are deeply involved in unrighteousness. These "leaders" (pastors) have been conditioned by unorthodox teaching to lay aside the particulars of belief as long as the name of God is used in order to promote the "Brotherhood of Man" religion.

The Bible teaches that we are to be a separate people, our foundation is in Jesus Christ alone, and our belief is in His shed blood for the redemption of sin, His virgin birth, and His bodily resurrection. We are to unite on these principles and separate ourselves from those who believe otherwise: "But though we, or an angel from heaven, preach any other gospel unto you than that which we have preached unto you, let him be accursed" (Galatians 1:8).

Even with good intentions, sincerity of heart, and

adherence to biblical standards, ministers of God's Word who are a part of the Masonic/Christian conflict through Masonic membership are plunging the Christian community into the prophetic brotherhood religion.

Paul wrote: "For other foundation can no man lay than that is laid, which is Jesus Christ" (1 Corinthians 3:11). And John 8:12 says: "Then spake Jesus again unto them, saying, I am the light of the world: he that followeth me shall not walk in darkness, but shall have the light of life."

CHAPTER
4

OATHS: BINDING
SANCTIONS

Freemasonry employs several different tactics to protect Lodge secrets and doctrine. This is accomplished not only by keeping secrets between degrees, but also by the intentional deception of lower-degree members. Degree oaths are also administered for this purpose. Many times warnings are imparted to dissuade members from considering the viewpoints of those who "attack" the Lodge.

A good cause for attack is not found in the Lodge's public acts of charity but in its veiled and distorted teaching about Jesus.

Evidence of such a warning is found in *Freemasonry's Attitude Toward Politics and Religion,* issued by the Grand Lodge of Illinois, 1949: "Probably we shall always be subject to attacks of one kind or another, but as long as we stick to Freemasonry and give no just cause for being attacked, our enemies will soon find their efforts wasted."

A good cause for attack is not found in the Lodge's public acts of charity but in its veiled and distorted teaching about Jesus, which is the factor that determines the nature and relationship of any group—friend or foe—with Christianity. The charitable acts performed by many Masons only deepen the deception. Many Masons, however, have recognized the conflict and the degradation brought to Christ and Christianity and have "come out" from among them.

46

If only one person were to be saved from Masonry, then all efforts would be rewarded.

The most common way Masons protect their organization is by requiring candidates to swear an oath that binds them to secrecy. The Mason must swear such an oath at least 26 times throughout the first three degrees (Blue Degrees). The punishments inflicted upon those who betray the promises of secrecy are violent and can include having the throat cut, the tongue torn out, the left breast torn open, the heart and vitals removed and eaten by wild beasts, the body being severed in two, and the bowels being burnt to ashes.

Encyclopedia of Freemasonry says this under the heading "Mysteries, Ancient":

> The esoteric character of the mysteries was preserved by the most powerful sanctions. An oath of secrecy was administered in the most solemn form to the initiate, and to violate it was considered a sacrilegious crime, the prescribed punishment for which was immediate death, and we have at least one instance in Livy of the infliction of the penalty (pg. 499).

The following oaths are generic and have been quoted from *Illustrations of Masonry* by Captain William Morgan (pgs. 21, 52, 73). The wording might differ from state to state or from Lodge to Lodge; however, the basics are maintained.

First Degree Oath (Apprentice Degree)
    I, _____, of my own free will and accord, in the

presence of Almighty God and this worshipful lodge of Free and Accepted Masons, dedicated to God, and held forth to the holy order of St. John, do hereby and hereon most solemnly and sincerely promise and swear that I will always hail, ever conceal and never reveal any part or parts, art or arts, point or points of the secret arts and mysteries of ancient Freemasonry, which I have received, am about to receive, or may hereafter be instructed in, to any person or persons in the known world, except it be to a true and lawful brother Mason, or within the body of a just and lawfully constituted lodge of such; and not unto him, nor unto them whom I shall hear so to be, but unto him and them only whom I shall find so to be after strict trial and due examination, or lawful information. Furthermore, do I promise and swear that I will not write, print, stamp, stain, hew, cut, carve, indent, paint, or engrave it on anything movable or immovable, under the canopy of heaven, whereby or whereon the least letter, figure, character, mark, stain, shadow, or resemblance of the same may become legible or intelligible of myself for any other persons in the known world, whereby the secrets of Masonry may be unlawfully obtained through my unworthiness. To all of which I do most solemnly and sincerely promise and swear, without the least equivocation, mental reservation, or self evasion of mind in me whatever; binding myself under no less penalty than to have my throat cut across, my tongue torn out by the roots, and my body buried in the rough sands of the sea at low-water mark, where the tide ebbs and flows twice in 24 hours; so help me God, and keep me steadfast in the due performance of the same.

The candidate is then asked: "Brother, what do you most desire?" The candidate responds: "Light."

Second-Degree Oath (Fellow-Craft Degree)

I, _____, of my own free will and accord, in the presence of Almighty God, and this worshipful lodge of Fellow-Craft Masons, dedicated to God, and held forth to the holy order of St. John, do hereby and hereon most solemnly and sincerely promise and swear, in addition to my former obligation, that I will not give the degree of a Fellow-Craft Mason to anyone of an inferior degree, nor to any other being in the known world, except it be to a true and lawful brother or brethren Fellow-Craft Masons, within the body of a just and lawfully constituted lodge of such; and not unto him and them only whom I shall hear so to be, but unto him and them only whom I shall find so to be after strict trial and due examination or lawful information. Furthermore, do I promise and swear that I will not wrong this lodge or a brother of this degree to the value of two cents, knowingly, myself, nor suffer it to be done by others if in my power to prevent it. Furthermore, do I promise and swear that I will support the Constitution of the Grand Lodge of this State, under which this lodge is held, and conform to all the by-laws, rules and regulations of this or any other lodge of which I may at any time hereafter become a member, as far as in my power. Furthermore, do I promise and swear that I will obey all regular signs and summonses given, handed, sent, or thrown to me by the hand of a brother Fellow-Craft Mason, or from the body of a just and lawfully constituted lodge of such, provided that it be within the length of my cable-tow, or square and angle of my work. Furthermore, do I promise and swear that I will be adding and assisting all poor and penniless brethren Fellow-Crafts, their widows and orphans, such, as far as in my power without injuring family or myself. To all which I do most solemnly and sincerely promise and swear without the least hesitation, mental reservation, or self evasion of mind in me whatever; binding myself under no less penalty than to have my breast torn open and my heart and vitals taken from thence and thrown over my left shoulder and carried into the valley of Jehosaphat, there to become a prey to the wild beasts of the field, and vulture of the air, if ever I should prove willfully guilty of violating any part of this my solemn oath or obligation of a Fellow-Craft Mason; so help me God, and keep me steadfast in the due performance of the same.

"Detach your hands and kiss the book, which is the Holy Bible, twice." And the Master says: "Brother, what do you most desire? The candidate answers his prompter: "Further light."

Third Degree Oath (Master Mason Degree)

I, _____, of my own free will and accord, in the presence of Almighty God and this worshipful lodge of Master Masons, dedicated to God, and held forth to the holy order of St. John, do hereby and hereon most solemnly and sincerely promise and swear, in addition to my former obligations, that I will not give the degree of a Master Mason to any of an inferior degree, nor to any other being in the known world, except it be to a true and lawful brother or brethren Master Masons, within the body of a just and lawfully constituted lodge of such; and not unto him nor

50

unto them whom I shall hear so to be, but unto him and them only whom I shall find so to be, after strict trial and due examination, or lawful information received. Furthermore, do I promise and swear, that I will not give the grand hailing sign of distress except I am in real distress, or for the benefit of the Craft when at work; and should I ever see that sign given or the word accompanying it, and the person who gave it appearing to be in distress I will fly to his relief at any risk of my life, should there be a greater probability of saving his life than losing my own. Furthermore, do I promise and swear that I will not wrong this lodge, or a brother of this degree to the value of one cent, knowingly, myself, or suffer it to be done by others, if in my power to prevent it. Furthermore, do I promise and swear, that I will not be at the initiating, passing and raising a candidate at one communication, without a regular dispensation from the Grand Lodge for the same. Furthermore, do I promise and swear that I will not be at the initiating, passing, or raising a candidate in a clandestine lodge, I knowing it to be such. Furthermore, do I promise and swear that I will not be at the initiating of any old man in dotage, a young man in nonage, an Atheist, irreligious libertine, idiot, mad-man, hermaphrodite, or woman. Furthermore, do I promise and swear that I will not speak evil of a brother Master Mason, neither behind his back nor before his face, but will apprise him of all approaching danger, if in my power. Furthermore, do I promise and swear that I will not violate the chastity of a Master Mason's wife, mother, sister, or daughter, I knowing them to be such, nor suffer it to be done by others, if in my power to prevent it. Furthermore, do I promise and swear that I will support the constitution of the Grand Lodge of the state of _____, under which the lodge is held, and conform to all the by-laws, rules, and regulations of this or any other lodge of which I may at any time hereafter become a member. Furthermore, do I promise and swear that I will obey all regular signs, summonses, or tokens given, handed, sent or thrown to me from the hand of a brother Master Mason, or from the body of a just and lawfully constituted lodge of such, provided it be within the length of my cable-tow. Furthermore, do I promise and swear that a Master Mason's secrets, given to me in charge as such, and I knowing them to be such, shall remain as secure and inviolable in my breast as in his own, when communicated to me, murder and treason excepted; and they left to my own election. Furthermore, do I promise and swear that I will go on a Master Mason's errand whenever required, even should I have to go bare-foot and bare-headed, if within the length of my cable-tow. Furthermore, do I promise and swear that I will always remember a brother Master Mason when on my knees offering up my devotions to Almighty God. Furthermore, do I promise and swear that I will be aiding and assisting all poor, indigent Master Masons, their wives and orphans, wheresoever [they may be] disposed around the globe, as far as in my power, without injuring myself or family materially. Furthermore do I promise and swear that if any part of my solemn oath or obligation is omitted at this time, that I will hold myself amenable thereto whenever informed. To all, which I do most sincerely promise and swear, with a fixed and steady purpose of mind in me to keep and perform the same, binding myself under no less penalty than to have my body severed in two in the midst, and divided to the north and south, my bowels burnt to ashes in the center, and the ashes scattered before the four winds of heaven, that there might not the least track or trace of remembrance remain among men or Masons, of so vile and perjured a wretch as I should be, were I ever to prove willfully guilty of violating any part of this my solemn oath or obligation of a Master Mason. So help me God, and keep me steadfast in the due performance of the same.

The Master then asks the candidate: "What do you most desire?" The candidate responds: "More light."

Ezekiel 21:23, Zechariah 5:3–4 and Jeremiah 23:10 are only a few Old Testament references that warn against swearing or binding oneself with an oath. New Testament warnings include:

• Matthew 5:33–37: "Again, ye have heard that it hath been said by them of old time, Thou shalt not forswear thyself, but shalt perform unto the Lord thine oaths: But I say unto you, Swear not at all; neither by heaven; for it is God's throne: Nor by the earth; for it is his footstool: neither by Jerusalem; for it is the city of the great King. Neither shalt thou swear by thy head, because thou canst not make one hair white or black. But let your communication be, Yea, yea; Nay, nay: for whatsoever is more than these cometh of evil."

• James 5:12: "But above all things, my brethren, swear not, neither by heaven, neither by the earth, neither by any other oath: but let your yea be yea; and your nay, nay; lest ye fall into condemnation."

So we see that being affiliated with the Masonic

Lodge is a very serious matter for the Christian to even consider because of the Bible's strict forbiddance of swearing oaths.

These oaths mention God's name in their impending penalties, a practice forbidden in Scripture: "Thou shalt not take the name of the LORD thy God in vain; for the LORD will not hold him guiltless that taketh his name in vain" (Exodus 20:7; Deuteronomy 5:11).

Many Masons claim these oaths are only "symbolic" and are not to be taken literally. It must be noted however, that these oaths are taken by saying, "So help me God, and keep me steadfast." In addition, when asked, "What makes you a Mason?" the answer is, "My obligation."

It is not in God's character to contradict His written Word. God does not compromise when it comes to oaths that bind us to those who do not accept Jesus Christ as Lord!

In his second letter to the Corinthians, the Apostle Paul wrote: "Be ye not unequally yoked together with unbelievers...or what part hath he that believeth in Jesus as Lord with an infidel?" (2 Corinthians 6:14-15).

In *Morals and Dogma,* we read: "Upon entering the Order, the initiate binds himself to every Mason in the world."

Conflict? Yes.

CHAPTER 5

MASONIC ROOTS: CHRIST, SOLOMON OR BAAL?

In previous chapters we learned that Freemasonry is a non-sectarian Order that embraces the principles of all religions. Such boasts of universality are a predominant theme woven throughout Masonic teaching. Although it encompasses a conglomeration of various religious principles, the Order must have a beginning, or roots from which it derived.

This chapter is devoted to investigating the roots of Freemasonry — not its flesh-and-blood lineage, but the source from where its philosophy is drawn, particularly the Third-Degree, which reveals where Masonry truly places its reverence.

Masons disagree about the origin of Masonry. This conflict may stem from personal resentments of evidence or from a number of other reasons. Therefore, only those sources that are deemed reliable will be used for reference.

Such boasts of universality are a predominant theme woven throughout Masonic teaching.

The first traces of Masonic reverence are found in Mackey and McClenachan's *Encyclopedia of Freemasonry*:

> The principles of Freemasonry preceded the advent of Christianity. Its symbols and its legends are derived from the Solomon Temple and from the people anterior to that. Its religion comes from the ancient priesthood, its faith was that primitive one of Noah and his immediate descendants (pg. 148).

This refers us to the legend of the Third-Degree ritual, which centers on King Solomon and Hiram, the widow's son.

We also see that these symbols and legends were derived from people who lived prior to the Solomon period, which refers to the ancient Egyptians and their god Osiris, to whom we shall later refer.

Freemason beliefs are said to have come from Noah and his immediate descendants. We will examine the chronology of Freemasonry beginning with Noah.

In the Old Testament book of Genesis we learn that only eight people survived the Flood of Noah's time and were expected to replenish the human race: Noah and his wife, their three sons and their wives: "These are the families of the sons of Noah, after their generations, in their nations: and by these were the nations divided in the earth after the flood" (Genesis 10:32). Since all nations of the world came from these eight people, it is evident that all philosophical beliefs and principles also originated from them.

The names of Noah's sons — Japheth, Ham and Shem — are listed in Genesis 10. Genesis 11:10–27 records Shem's lineage to Abram (Abraham). The New Testament provides the complete lineage from Abraham to Christ Jesus, revealing the Shemites or the Semitic lineage (that of flesh and blood) as designated by God to be His chosen people through whom Jesus would later come, the roots and instructional reference of the Christian faith.

As Christianity permeates every culture and race, flesh-and-blood lineage becomes irrelevant because Christ accepts all who come to Him to partake of His righteousness. Through the spiritual entity known as the Church (born-again believers), we become members of the spiritual house of Abraham (Galatians 3:26–29).

Christ accepts all who come to Him to partake of His righteousness.

It would be interesting if Freemasonry had its philosophical roots in the principles of the Shemite lineage; however, when compared to Christianity, the origins and the histories of the two entities are dissimilar (*Encyclopedia of Freemasonry*, pg. 148).

The only substantial evidence given in Masonry about Noah is the term "Noachidae," derived from the "legend of the Craft," which reveals that Noah was "the father and founder of the Masonic system of theology" (*Encyclopedia of Freemasonry*, pg. 514).

Masonic reference to Noah, however, is both fantasized and purely symbolic in nature, of which the following is proof:

> Such are the Noachic traditions of Masonry, which, though if considered as material of history, would be worth but little, yet have furnished valuable sources of symbolism, and in that way are full of wise instruction (*Encyclopedia of Freemasonry*, pg. 515).

Also in the *Encyclopedia of Freemasonry*, we read:

> After the death of Noah, his sons removed from the region of Mount Ararat, where, until then, they had resided, and 'traveling from the East, found a plain in the land of Shinar, and dwelt there.' Here they commenced the building of a lofty tower *(Encyclopedia of Freemasonry*, pg. 515).

In the biblical account, Shinar was the name of the land where the cities of Babylon, Erech, Accad, and Calneh were located. Babylon is derived from the root *balal* ("to confound" – Hebrew), and refers to the confusion of languages at the lofty tower mentioned above (Genesis 11:9).

Significance

Encyclopedia of Freemasonry relates the following information about Nimrod:

> The legend of the Craft in the Old Constitutions refers to Nimrod as one of the founders of Masonry. Thus in the York MS., No. 1, we read, 'At ye making of your toure of Babell there was a Masonrie first much esteemed of, and the King of Babilon yet called Nimrod was a Mason himself and loved well Masons (pg. 513).

Nimrod was the most outstanding leader during the time between the Flood and Abraham. An enterprising man, his widespread popularity is noted by the fact that several cities were named in connection to him, including Birs Nimrud; Tell Nimrud (near Baghdad); and the Mound of Nimrud (ancient Calah). He revealed his military might as being a "mighty hunter," and also is noted for his protectiveness at a time when wild animals were a continual menace. He was the first to build fenced or fortified cities (*Halley's Bible Handbook,* pg. 82).

Not only did Nimrod "love well the Masons," but they also esteemed him for his work in Masonry. Many Masons who profess to be Christians refer to Genesis 10:9, which refers to him as "mighty hunter before the LORD" to substantiate his greatness and virtue. However, a simple study of the sentiment behind this phrase reveals that what the Masons label as being his "virtue" is quite different than what is commonly accepted.

The word "mighty" (*gibbowr*, Hebrew) means a "warrior" or a "tyrant." A tyrant exercises power in a harsh and cruel manner. Nimrod is also known in history as a hunter of men. The latter part of the phrase "before the Lord" stems from the word "before," which comes from the Hebrew word *paniym*, meaning "the face" (as the part that turns). In other words, Nimrod was a tyrant who turned his face from the Lord, which is why the Hebrew people referred to him as a rebel.

Nimrod was a tyrant who turned his face from the Lord.

Ordinarily, the founder of many cities and nations was recognized as the citizens' chief god, which was the case with Nimrod. To make this "god" more real and more honorable, images were made to represent him. Later the images were worshipped. This also was true of certain constellations that were named for him after his death. As the chief god of Babylon and Nineveh, Nimrod had images that represented him. These images glorified his attributes as a knowledgeable protector, leader, and god of war.

God confused the languages during the building of the tower of Babel, an endeavor undertaken by Nimrod; the building of the structure was then stopped. The Bible says all the people in the entire world had spoken one language prior to this event (Genesis 11). But after the languages were confused, people could no longer use one name to call upon their god. Thus, Nimrod, their chief god, then became known by multiple names. Since Nimrod had so many events and traits attributed to him, it was only reasonable for people, now in segregation, to adopt the portion of belief that was best interpreted by each group. This resulted in diverse religious attributes and beliefs, yet the people remained reverent to their god.

Scripture gives the revered Nimrod many names. Chemosh, Molock, Merodach, Remphan, Tammuz, and Baal are only a few examples of the 38 biblical titles and the numerous representatives of these "gods."

An entry in *Halley's Bible Handbook* says, "Babylonia was long known as the 'Land of Nimrod.' And that he was afterward deified, his name being identical with Merodach" (pg. 82).

Tyndale's *New Bible Dictionary* identifies Merodach as "the Hebrew form of the Babylonian divine name Marduk. Marduk was the primary deity of Babylon and was later called by his epithet Bel (Ba'al), so that his defeat was synonymous with that of his people (Jeremiah 50:2) as was that of the earlier Canaanite Ba'al" (pg. 761).

Baal worship was a form of ancient sun worship.

Baal worship was a form of ancient sun worship, for Baal (Nimrod) was represented by the sun. Many names throughout biblical and classical history appear and refer to Nimrod. These form what is referred to as the "ancient mysteries."

What About Egypt?

In *Morals and Dogma,* Pike refers to the ancient mysteries and Freemasonry as being one and the same, with exceptions found only in that of progressive alterations (pg. 624). Naturally, an examination of each ancient mystery would be time consuming and is not necessary for this study; here we will deal solely with the mystery religion that Masonry declares as being true.

Encyclopedia of Freemasonry says:

> Egypt has always been considered as the birthplace of the mysteries. It was there that the ceremonies of initiation were first established. It was there that truth

62

was first veiled in allegory, and the dogmas of religion was first imparted under symbolic forms.

To Egypt, therefore, Masons have always looked with peculiar interest as the cradle of that mysterious science of symbolism whose peculiar modes of teaching they alone, of all modern institutions, have preserved to the present day (pg. 232).

We have learned that the Masonic "religion" comes from the ancient priesthood. One might think this refers to the Levitical priesthood described in the Bible; however, the priesthood of Egypt is the Lodge's reference:"The priesthood of Egypt constituted a sacred caste, in whom the sacerdotal functions were hereditary" (*Encyclopedia of Freemasonry*, pg. 232).

What is the Connection?

Although the idea of many gods stemmed from Nimrod and the confusion at the Tower of Babel, only certain ones (those in exalted positions) were represented by the sun and moon. In *Morals and Dogma* we read: "We know that the Egyptians worshipped the sun, under the name of Osiris" (pg. 406).

Pike connects Baal worship and Osiris as being identical:

The Goths had three festivals; the most magnificent of which commenced at the winter solstice, and was celebrated in honor of Thor, the Prince of the Power of the Air...Thor was the Sun, the Egyptian Osiris and Kneph, the Phoenician Bel or Baal. The initiations were had in huge intricate caverns, terminating, as all the Mithriac caverns did, in a spacious vault, where the candidate was brought to light (*Morals and Dogma,* pg. 368).

The legend of Egyptian god Osiris is significant to Masonry because of the Third-Degree ritual and other teachings that are deeply rooted in Egyptian legend. This legend and the legend of Hiram Abiff, a ritual familiar to all Third-Degree Masons, contains similarities that cannot be overlooked.

The Legend of Osiris

Osiris was the chief god of Egypt, the son and husband of Isis. His jealous brother Typhon had supposedly killed Osiris by trickery. Osiris was nailed in a chest and cast into the Nile. Later, his dead body was cast up at Byblos in Phoenicia and left at the foot of a tamarind tree. Isis retrieved his body only to lose it again to the jealous brother who then cut him into 14 pieces, which he scattered around the kingdom. Again Isis went to search for Osiris and found all of his body parts except his phallus, which had been

Osiris was the chief god of Egypt, the son and husband of Isis.

eaten by a crab in the Nile. Isis then made a phallus, which was to be sacred (origin of the obelisk). She embalmed him, thus claiming restoration and giving rise to the concept that the immortality of the soul is dependent on the preservation of the body. Osiris was afterward known as the lord of the underworld. He was also god of the sun and god of fertility, worshipped in orgiastic sex rituals.

Third-Degree Masonic Ritual

As Masonry has preserved the Egyptian science of symbolism, it is apparent that an observation or ritual exists that projects from Egypt; thus, the ritual of the Third-Degree or Master Mason Degree. This ritual however, is presumed to be centered on the account of King Solomon and Hiram: Hiram of Tyre, a widow's son, was working on Solomon's temple when three ruffians desirous of the master's word approached him. Hiram refused on three occasions to give the word and was killed by the third ruffian, who cast a blow to Hiram's forehead with a setting maul. Hiram was then buried in the temple until midnight, when the ruffians returned to take his body (westerly) to bury him again. The following day, they found him missing and the Craft, in confusion, required the cause. The workmen had already searched for Hiram but without success. Thus, King Solomon sent out a party again to search for him. Upon returning after several days of searching, members of the search party stopped to rest and refresh themselves. They accidentally discovered Hiram's freshly dug grave beneath an acacia tree. At this time they heard lamenting at a nearby cleft, the self-impending penalties (same as oath penalties) of the ruffians Jubela, Jubelo, and Jubelum. Thus, the search was over and the murderers were caught.

After a preliminary ritual, the candidate for the

This raising of the candidate is meant to symbolize the resurrection, which is the object of the degree.

Third-Degree initiation is found lying on the floor, which represents the death of Hiram. The junior warden holds the candidate's right hand and attempts to "raise" him from the dead, but without success. His hand slips from the candidate's hand, symbolizing an insufficient grip.

The senior warden then makes a failed attempt due symbolically to the flesh cleaving from the bone. Again, it is an insufficient grip.

Representing King Solomon, the Worshipful Master successfully raises the candidate using the "Strong Grip" or the "Lion's Paw Grip." The candidate is raised on the five points of fellowship:

1) foot to foot
2) knee to knee
3) breast to breast
4) hand to back
5) cheek to cheek

In this position the Master gives the Grand Masonic Word — *Mah-HaH-Bone*. This raising of the candidate is meant to symbolize the resurrection, which is the object of the degree (*Mah-HaH-Bone*) – Hebrew: "What! The builder?"

Of course, this ritual has a Christian interpretation,

which Pike explains:

> The murder of Hiram, his burial, and his being raised again by the Master, are symbols, both of the death, burial, and resurrection of the Redeemer; and of the death and burial in sins of the natural man, and his being raised again to a new life, or born again, by the direct action of the Redeemer (*Morals and Dogma*, pg. 640).

We must note that the above ritual is only symbolic as it is stated here; that is, it is not the actual thing. We must also remember that the Blue Degrees (first three) are intentionally misled by false interpretation; thus, this ritual does not actually refer to Hiram, especially when compared to the biblical account.

Masonic teaching claims Hiram died "during the work," yet the Bible says he (Huram) "finished the work" and mentions nothing about his death and miraculous recovery at the hand of Solomon. We also find that this was God's house and not Solomon's.

Second Chronicles 4:11 says: "And Huram made the pots, and the shovels, and the basons. And Huram finished the work that he was to make for king Solomon for the house of God."

When the legends of Osiris and Hiram are compared, we learn that both died at the hand of a brother; both were searched for twice; both were found at the foot of a tree; and both suffered a loss. Osiris was missing a body part and the master's word was lost.

The following information says the Third-Degree

ritual is not actually that of Hiram or of Christ, but is the legend of Osiris. Thus, in the Third-Degree of Masonry, the initiate actually enters the death, burial, and resurrection of Osiris. Speaking of the Degree of "Knight of the Brazen Serpent," we read:

> While it teaches the necessity of reformation as well as repentance, as a means of obtaining mercy and forgiveness, it is also devoted to an explanation of the symbols of Masonry; and especially to those which are connected with that ancient and universal legend of which that of Khir-Om Abi is but a variation; that legend which, representing a murder or a death, and a restoration to life, by a drama, which figure Osiris, Isis and Horus...and many another representatives of active and passive powers of nature, taught the Initiates in the Mysteries that the rule of Evil and Darkness is but temporary, and that that of Light and Good will be eternal (*Morals and Dogma,* pg. 435). [note: "Khir-Om Abi" – "Hiram Abiff"]

In Chapter One we learned that the "raised" candidate is supposedly raised into a philosophy of regeneration, or the new birth of all things. This philosophy, as that of Egypt, reveals the worship or exaltation of nature. Pike wrote this about nature and Osiris: "Everything good in nature comes from Osiris" (*Morals and Dogma,* pg. 476).

This typifies not only life out of death, but the regeneration of the things of nature or 'generative power' (sexual reproductive power). In addition, "Osiris and Isis were the sun and moon, is attested by many ancient writers, which, as we have seen, refers

68

to Baal or Nimrod, one of the founders of Masonry. Thus Osiris, Nimrod, Baal, Merodach, etc. are synonymous; that is, they are one and the same. Masonic reverence of the sun is a familiar practice to all Masons, even if unknowingly, in the symbol of the All-Seeing Eye: The sun was termed by the Greeks as the Eye of Jupiter, and the Eye of the World; and his is the All-Seeing Eye in our Lodges" (*Morals and Dogma*, pgs. 476, 477).

Speaking of those of Thebes, an ancient city in Upper Egypt, Pike notes: "Soon they personified the sun, and worshipped him under the name of Osiris, and

Many Masons today are duped into practicing the same Baal worship of biblical times.

transmuted the legend of his descent among the winter signs, into a fable of his death, his descent into the infernal regions, and his resurrection" (pg. 447).

It is noteworthy to mention that the officers at the opening of Lodge ceremonies — Worshipful Master, senior and junior wardens — are seated at stations in the east, south and west. In the religious symbolism of Freemasonry, the sun is represented as "his" rising, "his" meridian, and "his" setting.

Many Masons today are duped into practicing the same Baal worship of biblical times. They are told the All-Seeing Eye represents God, as does the letter "G". The name "God," however, is mistaken in quite the same way as the name "Baal" in the Old Testament.

The name "Baal" meant "lord" or "possessor," which, by name, was easily mistaken for the God of Abraham, who is also called "Lord." But the manner in which each was worshipped was quite different and the differences become obvious when compared. Such is the Masonic/Christian conflict!

After God confused the languages at the Tower of Babel, Nimrod became known by multiple names and by different attributes. These names and attributes were adapted by different cultures of the people who were dispersed from Shinar, where the tower was located. In the centuries that followed, philosophers began to recognize the similarities in worship and reverence through subsequent studies of these cultures. It was only natural for elite philosophers to recognize the most elaborate and dogmatic of these people from whom to draw their assumptions. Egypt was that main source, especially for Freemasonry, for Freemasonry is a speculative search: "The history of Masonry is the history of Philosophy" (*Morals and Dogma*, pg. 540).

The roots of Freemasonry lie in Egyptian legend with reverence to Osiris or Baal (Nimrod); thus, it is actual Baal worship.

Its faith is indeed that primitive one of Noah and his immediate descendants, particularly Nimrod, who was deified under the names Merodach, Baal, Osiris, etc. The Solomon legend was conjured in order for Christians to appear adaptable, for Solomon never raised anyone from death to life. The only possibility of this was through symbolism, when Solomon did "evil in the sight of the Lord."

"Then did Solomon build an high place for Chemosh, the abomination of Moab, in the hill that is before Jerusalem, and for Molech, the abomination of the children of Ammon. And likewise did he for all his strange wives, which burnt incense and sacrificed unto their gods" (1 Kings 11:7–8).

The tribes of Israel were often seduced into worshipping Nimrod (Baal, Osiris) not only because of the confusing name "Baal," but due largely to their bondage in Egypt. As a nation, Israel is said to have had its birth as a nation in its exodus from Egypt. During the Israelites' time in bondage, they multiplied in number under the influences of Egyptian custom and worship.

Following their exodus from Egypt, the gaiety and licentious character of the Egyptian god was soon revealed in the absence of their leader, Moses, who had gone up Mt. Sinai to receive the Ten Commandments from the Lord. When Moses returned he found the Israelites worshipping a golden calf, an Egyptian image symbolizing Osiris and regenerative power.

Smith's Bible Dictionary defines the word "calf" as an "image for worship made at Sinai in imitation of the Apis (Mnevis?) of Egypt, from the jewelry borrowed of the Egyptians (Ex.xxxii.2). Not of solid gold, but of wood, gilded and plated with gold (as the emblem of Osiris-Apis was made)."

71

The Israelites were supposed to worship the God of Abraham, Isaac, and Jacob, not the "gods" of the surrounding people. Scripture contains many instances where the Israelites were explicitly warned against such idolatrous behavior. Moses undoubtedly recognized the symbol since Pharaoh's daughter raised him and he "was learned in all the wisdom of the Egyptians" (Acts 7:22). In a fit of anger, Moses broke the stone tablets that contained the Ten Commandments. The Israelites' idolatry caused the death of approximately 3,000 people. In addition, "the LORD plagued the people, because they made the calf, which Aaron made" (Exodus 32:35). The calf was always a bull with horns, which represented sexual strength or regenerative power. Paganism is always sexual in its outworking and results ultimately in phallus worship.

The Israelites were supposed to worship the God of Abraham, Isaac, and Jacob, not the "gods" of the surrounding people.

Time and again Israel was seduced into participating in such worship (Deuteronomy 13:6,7). In one fashion or another, many representatives were those of the false god Baal (Nimrod, Osiris). The Canaanite gods, Assyrian gods, the gods of the Ammorites and Moabites were only a few of the strange gods being worshipped.

In *Unger's Bible Dictionary*, under the heading "Idolatry" and subheading "Among the Ten Tribes of

72

Israel," we read: "Jeroboam, fresh from his recollections of the Apis worship of Egypt, erected golden calves at Bethel and Dan, and by this crafty state policy severed effectively the kingdoms of Judah and Israel" (1 Kings 12:26–33). [Note: Apis, the bull was also a symbol of Nimrod's strength.] (pg. 514).

Christian Concern

None of the many fallacies throughout our land can ever effectively topple Christianity. The Church is affected only when such outside influences are allowed to filter into Christian congregations through the avenues of church memberships, commissions, and leadership positions. Freemasonry is not an outside influence; it is an inside influence!

Freemasonry is not an outside influence; it is an inside influence!

As Jeroboam effectively severed Judah and Israel, Freemasonry slowly severs the Christian witness. Baal worship still exists! Satan is again using the oldest strategy in the world: Conquer the enemy from within to best conquer him from without.

Joshua wrote: "Now therefore fear the LORD, and serve him in sincerity and in truth: and put away the gods which your fathers served on the other side of the flood, and in Egypt; and serve ye the LORD. And if it seem evil unto you to serve the LORD, choose you this day whom ye will serve; whether the gods which your fathers served that were on the other side of the flood, or the gods of the Amorites, in whose land ye dwell: but as for me and my house, we will serve the LORD" (24:14–15).

CHAPTER
6

FREEMASONRY AND THE LUCIFERIAN CONNECTION

Satan's devices are as varied and numerous as the grains of sand on the seashore. His objective is always the same: conquer and divide. He used this strategic move in the Garden of Eden to cause division between Adam and Eve to achieve his ultimate goal, separating man from God, which he accomplished by presenting the spiritual idealism that man can choose his own way and become his own god. The forbidden fruit was the instrument Satan chose to use for this particular deception.

Satan's objective is always the same: conquer and divide.

In its most spiritual and ancient form, Freemasonry has been the forbidden fruit for God's people since before the Tower of Babel. We have seen how Masonry draws from the mystery religions and how Masonic rituals still propagate paganism. We have also seen that many Masons hold governing positions in evangelical churches. This infiltration has wounded many congregations. Moreover, many church buildings have been used for Lodge purposes. At one church, the Lodge had replaced the Christian symbol on the church steeple with a statue of a goat. The goat, a symbol not uncommon in Masonry, represents Baphomet, defined in the *Dictionary of Mysticism and the Occult* as a "demonic deity represented by Eliphas Levi as a goat-headed god with wings, breasts, and an illuminated torch between his horns" (pg. 24).

Baphomet is defined in the *Encyclopedia of Freemasonry* as follows:

> It will not be uncharitable or unreasonable to suggest that the Baphomet, or skull of ancient Templars, was, like the relic of their modern Masonic representatives, simply an impressive symbol teaching the lesson of morality, and that the latter has really been derived from the former (pg. 97).

We have established that the god of Freemasonry is not the God of the Bible. We have seen how Freemasonry honors and indeed worships Baal by many different names, one of which is Osiris (Nimrod). The god of Nimrod was not the Hebrews, but the fallen angel, Lucifer. Masonry is patterned after the mystery religions, which sprang from Nimrod and his mother/wife Semiramis, as well as the Tower of Babel. Lucifer is the god of Freemasonry. This claim is substantiated by Masonic author Manly P. Hall, 33rd–degree Mason, Knights Templar, in his book, *The Lost Keys of Freemasonry*:

The god of Nimrod was not the God of the Hebrews but the fallen angel, Lucifer.

> When the Mason learns that the key to the warrior on the block is the proper application of the dynamo of living power, he has learned the mystery of his Craft. The seething energies of Lucifer are in his hands and before he may step onward and upward, he must prove his ability to properly apply energy (pg. 48).

In his instructions of July 14, 1889 to the 23 Supreme Councils of the World, Albert Pike, Grand Commander, Sovereign Pontiff of Universal Freemasonry, stated the following:

To you, Sovereign Grand Inspectors General, we say this; that you may repeat it to the Brethren of the 32nd, 31st, and 30th degrees — the Masonic Religion should be, by all of us initiates of the high degrees, maintained in the purity of the Luciferian Doctrine.

If Lucifer were not God, would Adonay [the God of the Christians] whose deeds prove his cruelty, perfidy and hatred of man, barbarism and repulsion for science, would Adonay and his priests, calumniate him?

Yes, Lucifer is God, and unfortunately Adonay is also God. For the eternal law is that there is no light without shade, no beauty without ugliness, no white without black, for the absolute can only exist as two gods: darkness being necessary for light to serve as its foil as the pedestal is necessary to the statue, and the brake to the locomotive.

Thus, the doctrine of Satanism is a heresy; and the true and pure philosophical religion is the belief in Lucifer, the equal of Adonay; but Lucifer, God of Light and God of Good, is struggling for humanity against Adonay, the God of Darkness and Evil" (pg.588; recorded by A.C. De La Rive, La Femme et l'Enfant dans la Franc-Maconnerie Universelle).

God pronounced six woes upon Israel (Isaiah 5:20) because of their personal and national sins. The new morality of the day included those who were glorifying the bad and bashing the good. This type of role reversal is commonplace among the mystery religions and is immediately detected within the previous quote. The God of the Christian is Adonai,

———— () ————

The God of the Christian is Adonai, which means "Jehovah our Ruler."

which means "Jehovah our Ruler." Our enemy is Lucifer, the light-bearer-turned-adversary, who is the god of this world (Isaiah 14:12; Ephesians 2:2).

The Mormon "Brotherhood" of Jesus and Lucifer

Masonic authority Albert Pike equates Lucifer with Adonai. Mormonism, which is a stepchild of Freemasonry, also teaches that Lucifer and Jesus are spirit-brothers. Mormonism founder Joseph Smith was a Mason who adapted much Masonic lore and practice (paganism) into his newfound religion. The Mormon belief on the brotherhood of Jesus and Lucifer is explained in a discourse delivered by Brigham Young on October 30, 1870, in which we read:

> 'Who will redeem the earth, who will go forth and make the sacrifice for the earth and all things it contains?' The Eldest son [Jesus] said: 'Here am I'; and then he added, 'Send me.' But the second one [other son], which was 'Lucifer, Son of the Morning,' said, 'Lord, here am I, send me. I will redeem every son and daughter of Adam and Eve that lives on the earth, or that ever goes on the earth' (*Journal of Discourses*, Volume 13, pg. 283).

Mormons use their belief in the spiritual brother-hood of Jesus and Lucifer to explain the beginning of the great conflict between good and evil. In short, this conflict is between brothers. Joseph Smith's "theology" has led millions to accept Lucifer's leadership by Freemasonry's paganism. Mormons do not recognize Jesus as God but as one of God's spirit-children created by the "Father" and

( )

Joseph Smith's "theology" has led millions to accept Lucifer's leadership by Freemasonry's paganism.

"Mother" of heaven, which is a take on the Nimrod and Semiramis story we read earlier. The Mormons claim that Jesus was created through sexual relations between *Elohim* (God – *Adonai*) and Mary; that Jesus was married; and that His death on the cross does not provide full atonement for sin, but does provide everyone with resurrection. Again, the tenets of Freemasonry paganism, and indeed the legend of Nimrod and Semiramis, are deeply entrenched in Mormonism while its members say they are follow-ing Jesus Christ. This deception runs deep and it is sad.

Jesus *is* God; He is the Creator of heaven and earth. How could the Creator of the universe be the brother of His own creation? Jesus created the angels of heaven (Colossians 1:16–17), which included Lucifer, the anointed cherub who fell from heaven because of his pride and jealousy (Isaiah 14:12-15;

80

Luke 10:18). Lucifer the "light-bearer" is later referred to as Satan the "adversary." The Apostle Paul wrote these words about the creation and its Creator: "For by him [Jesus] were all things created, that are in heaven, and that are in earth, visible and invisible, whether they be thrones, or dominions, or principalities, or powers: all things were created by him, and for him: And he is before all things, and by him all things consist" (Colossians 1:16–17). "And without controversy great is the mystery of godliness: God was manifest in the flesh, justified in the Spirit, seen of angels, preached unto the Gentiles, believed on in the world, received up into glory" (1 Timothy 3:16).

The spirit of Freemasonry is not the Holy Spirit of the Bible. Freemasonry is a spiritual entity that has a profound influence and brings millions into spiritual bondage. The Bible warns: "Beloved, believe not every spirit, but try the spirits, whether they are of God: because many false prophets are gone out into the world" (1 John 4:1).

We test the spirits by the Word of God. The Bible teaches us that two opposing spirits cannot exist together in truth (2 Corinthians 6:15). Men of integrity should not try to straddle the fence, whether it is through involvement in a governmental position in a church body or by church membership alone. A man will either worship the God of the Bible in spirit and in truth or he will not (James 4:4). If a man professes that Christ is Lord while he is simultaneously a member of the Masonic Lodge, then he is living a deceptive, double life. Lucifer is resurrected when attempts are made to serve the risen Lord while continuing such a contradictory lifestyle. "Riding the goat" is the Freemason equivalent of "straddling the fence." Baphomet, the goat symbol of Freemasonry, represents the demonic deity of paganism and is a representative of Lucifer. *Encyclopedia of Freemasonry* says:

> As Dr. Oliver says, it was in England a common belief that Freemasons were accustomed "to raise the Devil." So the "riding of the goat," which was believed to be practiced by the witches, was transferred to the Freemasons; and the saying remains to this day although the belief has very long since died (pg. 301)

The Apostle Paul called this type of spirituality a "form of godliness" (2 Timothy 3:5). This is nothing more than a form of spiritual bondage. Lucifer the light-bearer, who became Satan, is also known in Scripture as the Devil. To exalt this light-bearer-turned-adversary is to exalt the Devil. Whatever the phrase "raising the Devil" has come to mean in today's Lodges, Masons are indeed "riding the goat" by exalting the Devil. (We will see more connections with witchcraft later in our study.)

The Hebrew shepherds treasured the goat because it was a very useful animal; they drank its milk, ate its flesh, and wove its hair into rough cloth. They used the animal's skin to make bottles for transporting water and wine. Goats often grazed with the sheep in mixed flocks, but unlike sheep, the goats were independent, willful, and curious. In the Old Testament, goats were sometimes used to symbolize irresponsible leadership (Jeremiah 50:8; Zechariah 10:3). This remains the case today, as expressed in those Masons who hold governmental positions among God's people, to whom the Bible refers as "sheep."

We cannot have it both ways: We are either in Christ or we are not.

Jesus used the goat in His teaching concerning the judgment of the nations (Matthew 25:32–33) to illustrate the ungodly, who cannot enter His kingdom. The Bible explains that not all who say "Lord, Lord" will enter into the kingdom of heaven (Matthew 7:21). We cannot have it both ways: We are either in Christ or we are not. Jesus stated: "Not everyone that saith unto me, Lord, Lord, shall enter into the kingdom of heaven; but he that doeth the will of my Father which is in heaven" (Matthew 7:21). He also said, "He that is not with me is against me; and he that gathereth not with me scattereth abroad" (Matthew 12:30).

FREEMASONRY AND ISLAM

Islam was founded in 610 AD. The Koran, Islam's Scripture, is not another version of the Bible, but a compilation of various writings collected from pieces of papyrus, flat stones, animal bones, pieces of leather, wooden boards or whatever was handy when Mohammed fell into one of his many trances. It is believed that the angel Gabriel — considered by Muslims to be the Holy Spirit — revealed these "visions" to Mohammed.

Those who follow Islam are called Muslims. To the Muslim, Jesus is one of the 124,000 prophets God sent to various cultures. He is seen as a "spirit" of God but not God in the flesh, as clearly taught in the Bible. According to Islam, Jesus was not crucified for the sins of the world but ascended to heaven without dying. Muslims believe that Jesus will return in the future to live and die.

According to Islam, Jesus was not crucified for the sins of the world but ascended to heaven without dying.

The five pillars of Islam are:
1) To confess that Allah is the one true God;
2) To recognize Mohammed as Allah's prophet;
3) To pray five times a day facing Mecca and to make a pilgrimage there at least once in a lifetime;
4) To give money for the progression of Islam;
5) To fast during Ramadan.

The Shrine Club is the Islamic expression of Freemasonry.

Islamic doctrine is clearly contrary to what the Bible teaches. True Christians would be appalled if someone suggested that the tenets of Islam should be integrated into their churches, or that practicing Muslims should be allowed to become members. Believers would immediately recognize that such an unbiblical inclusion would pollute the doctrine of Christ and cause strife and discord among the members of the congregation. Many church bodies, however, have unknowingly supported the tenets of Islam. How? Consider the Islamic roots of the Shrine Club.

The Shrine Club is known internally as the "Ancient Arabic Order, Nobles of the Mystic Shrine" (A.A.O.N.M.S.). The term "Ancient Arabic" should ring a bell. The Shrine Club is the Islamic expression of Freemasonry. (All Shriners are Masons, but not all Masons are Shriners.) What's wrong with this picture? Islamic doctrine directly contradicts Christian doctrine. The god of Islam is not the God of the Bible. Imagine if the pastor, a deacon, an elder or a member of your church revealed that he also followed Islam! What would you think?

Every Shriner takes an oath of obligation (a bloody death oath) kneeling before an Islamic altar upon which the Koran is displayed. The candidate seals his oath by calling upon "Allah, the God of the Arab, God of Mohammed and the God of my fathers," and confesses in the ritual, "he who follows Islam follows truth." (Is it any wonder Islam is gaining such momentum and acceptance today?) It's a sad fact, but many church members are also members of the Shrine Club, which means they support Islam. If a person wishes to remain a Mason, even a Shriner, he must separate himself from the church he attends. Well-known evangelist D.L. Moody said this about Masonic membership in general:

> I do not see how any Christian, most of all a Christian minister, can go into these secret lodges with unbelievers. They say they can have more influence for good, but I say that they can have more influence for good by staying out of them and reproving their evil deeds. You can never reform anything by unequally yoking yourself to ungodly men. True reformers separate themselves from the world. But, some say to me, if you talk that way you will drive all the members of secret societies out of your meetings and out of your churches. But what if I did? Better men will take their places. Give them the truth any-way, and if they would rather leave their churches than their lodges, the sooner they get out of their churches the better. I would rather have ten members who are separated from the world than a thousand such members! Come out from the lodge. Better one with God than a thousand without Him! We must walk with God, and if only one or two go with us, it is all right. Do not let down the standard to suit men who love their secret lodges or have some darling sin they will not give up! (*Freemasonry,* by Jack Harris, pgs. 109–110).

The Worship of Allah

Think about a man who professes to believe in Christ, enters the Shrine Club, kneels before an Islamic altar and professes Allah as the God of his fathers. Allah is a pre-Islamic deity, an Arab god and one of many Mecca deities. Allah worship was an astral religion that revered the sun, the moon, and the stars. We learned the various names designated for Baal and the different methods of worship in Chapter Five (Osiris, Nimrod, etc.). Allah is just another name for Baal and Islam is just another form of Baal worship. It is the worship of Nimrod (Baal/Bel), who transcended to the sun. While the moon was generally worshipped in the Ancient Near East as a female deity and the sun as male, the Arabs viewed the moon as a male deity (Allah) because of the influence of their prophet Mohammed. According to the book *Islamic Invasion,* we read: "Allah is a pre-Islamic name...corresponding to the Babylonian Bel" (pg. 48).

Allah is just another name for Baal and Islam is just another form of Baal worship.

The Shrine Club is one of the ploys Satan uses to divide from within to conquer the whole. I am well aware that Shrine hospitals have helped many children and I am overjoyed to see that these children are being helped; however, we must consider the complete picture and the religious ties of the Order, not merely their outward expressions. Although helping crippled children is commendable and touches our hearts, we must pay attention to what is being veiled behind these good works.

The following article appeared in a 1986 issue of the *Orlando Sentinel:*

> Shrine literature refers to the hospitals as the soul of the Shrine and the reason for Shrinedom. Yet Internal Revenue Service records indicate that the Shrine, the nation's richest charity, gives its 22 Shriners hospitals for crippled children less than a third of the millions of dollars it raises from the public each year.
>
> Estimates from available records also show that Shrine hospitals in 1984 received just 1 percent, or $182,000, of an estimated $17.5 million in profits from about 175 circuses (June 29, 1986, pg. A–15).

Many professing Christians who are members of the Shrine Club stand at highway intersections and collect donations for the Shrine. A large percentage of these donations help support Shrine parties (Shriners are known as "the party animals" of Freemasonry), drunkenness, and a number of other such sins. Yet pastors, deacons, or church members collect these funds to support such corruption. Imagine these same men on Sunday mornings speaking out against the very activities for which they collected money. These funds also have supplied many perks for the potentates, including jewelry, gifts, and trips (plus expenses), which are given to those who secure high offices. The money collected at these highway intersections and through sales of circus tickets supports the same activities and behaviors.

The Peculiar Red Hat

Not only has Freemasonry supported Islam through its membership in the Shrine Club, but it also includes another link with the Islamic faith: The Masons wear a peculiar red hat called a "fez," which just happens to be the traditional head covering for Muslims. These hats were not always red. The explanation for the red color appears to have its origin in blood – literally.

Islam was borne from a military conquest and has historically recruited converts with the sword. Mohammed said, "The sword is the key of heaven and hell." The incompatibility of Islam and Christianity cannot be more clearly seen than in the history of the fez.

In 800 AD, Muslims overran the Christian city of Fez in Morocco in a westward sweep of Islam that resulted in the slaughter of approximately 50,000 men, women, and children. The blood of the murdered Christians ran into the streets. The Muslim conquerors celebrated the slaughter by dipping their woolen caps into the blood, which turned them red, and then they wore them to symbolize their victory. Apparently, this is the origin of both the name (fez) and the color (red) of the cap.

Whether he knows it or not, every Shriner who dons a red fez is actually commemorating the slaughter of thousands of Christians. Doesn't it seem rather odd that the Islamic expression of Freemasonry conducts itself under the ploy of supporting children? (For more on this and other secular practices, visit Tom McKenney's "Words for Living Ministries" website at www.wordsforliving.org).

Furthermore, the crescent moon and the sword are universal symbols of Islam. These symbols honor Allah, the god of the Muslims, as well as represent the blood shed in his name. These symbols are displayed on Shriner buildings, automobiles, hats and other articles. The use of the crescent moon as the symbol for Islam, seen on the flags of Islamic nations and on the top of mosques and minarets, is a throwback to the days when Allah was worshipped in Mecca as the moon god. Surely Muslims must shake

Whether he knows it or not, every Shriner who dons a red fez is actually commemorating the slaughter of thousands of Christians.

their heads and laugh when they see professing Christians flagrantly display symbols that represent Allah. Again, the one who says he is a Christian but remains in the Lodge needs to make a choice: Leave the church or leave the Lodge! The Bible says: "Be ye not unequally yoked together with unbelievers: for what fellowship hath righteousness with unrighteousness? And what communion hath light with darkness? And what concord hath Christ with

Belial? Or what part hath he that believeth with an infidel? And what agreement hath the temple of God with idols? For ye are the temple of the living God; as God hath said, I will dwell in them, and walk in them; and I will be their God, And they shall be my people. Wherefore come out from among them, and be ye separate, saith the Lord, and touch not the unclean thing; and I will receive you, And will be a Father unto you, and ye shall be my sons and daughters, saith the Lord Almighty" (2 Corinthians 6:14–18).

CHAPTER
8

THE EASTERN STAR:
BINDING THE
MASONIC FAMILY

The paganism of the Masonic Lodge has not only weakened our church fellowship and spiritual effectiveness over the years but it has brought many children and grandchildren into spiritual bondage. Many sons and daughters of church-affiliated Masons will have nothing to do with a church. This is not an across-the-board fact but a rule of thumb. This disassociation from the church could likely be the result of a generational curse brought upon the children of Masons. (See Exodus 34:7 for the biblical teaching that states that sin, regardless of its type, will in one form or another be "visited" upon the children of those who commit such sins.) Thankfully, there are exceptions to the tendency of children of Masons to stay away from church; some sons and daughters of Masons who come to Christ break — or never make — ties with the Lodge, in effect breaking the generational curse of such paganism.

Entire families are held in spiritual bondage when the head of the household is a Lodge member.

Entire families are held in spiritual bondage when the head of the household is a Lodge member. This becomes even more obvious when we look at the involvement of women in the Lodge. The Order of the Eastern Star was specifically designed to include women in Masonry. *Encyclopedia of Freemasonry* describes the Eastern Star as:

The very popular American Rite of Adoption to which Brother Robert Morris gave many years' labor and dedicated numerous poems. There are five beautiful degrees to which Freemasons and their mothers, wives, sisters and daughters are eligible. The ceremonies are entirely different to the old Rites of Adoption practiced on the continent of Europe (pg. 227).

The five degrees of the Eastern Star are:

Corruption breeds only corruption (Luke 6:43).

1) Jephthah's Daughter, the daughter's degree (she is called Adah by the Eastern Star);
2) Ruth, the widow's degree;
3) Esther, the wife's degree;
4) Martha, the sister's degree;
5) Electra, the benevolent degree.

The obvious reason the Lodge implemented the Eastern Star as part of Adoptive Masonry is that female relatives had become a hindrance to the furtherance of Lodge practice. The men were prohibited from sharing Lodge secrets, which obviously caused a problem. The solution: Include the women. This inclusion has only strengthened the pagan grip and spiritual bondage for the entire family. If the parents are corrupt, the offspring will also be corrupt. Corruption breeds only corruption (Luke 6:43).

In many instances the Eastern Star is referred to as

female Masonry; however, a woman cannot actually become a Mason. Under the heading "Adoptive Masonry, American" in the *Encyclopedia of Freemasonry*, we read:

> The last phase of this female Masonry to which our attention is directed is the system of androgynous degrees, which are practiced to some extent in the United States...When a woman is informed that, by passing through the brief and unimpressive ceremony of any one of these degrees, she has become a Mason, the deception is still more gross and inexcusable (pg. 29).

Thus, the Eastern Star is inferior to the Masonic Lodge and must be governed or overseen by men from the Lodge:

> This appellation is derived from the fact that every female or Adoptive Lodge is obliged, by the regulations of the association, to be, as it were, adopted by, and thus placed under the guardianship of, some regular Lodge of Freemasons (*Encyclopedia of Freemasonry*, pg. 24).

The Order of the Eastern Star is androgynous— that is, it is for both male and female—with the men presiding over the women. For a man to become a part of the Eastern Star, he must at the least be a Master Mason (Third Degree) in good standing with the Lodge. A woman may only join if she has a close relative who is a Master Mason and if she is the proper age.

The Eastern Star Motto

"We have seen His star in the East, and are come to worship Him." This may look like Matthew 2:2 from the Bible, but it is actually a Masonic adaptation of the verse. However, in accordance with the nature of the beast that presides over them, this too, is deceptive. It is common for the learned of Freemasonry to attach themselves to the wisdom of the Gnostics; hence, their attachment to the "wise men" of Matthew 2:2. Many Masonic authors have labored furiously to connect the magi (wise men) to their Order. This is done in an effort to substantiate a justifiable connection to our Lord for the benefit of the Eastern Star. Moreover, some have ventured to connect the magi with magic, which is a topic of study for many Masons.

Many Masonic authors have labored furiously to connect the magi (wise men) to their Order.

> Much light, it must be confessed, is thrown on many of the mystical names in the higher degrees by the dogmas of magic; and hence magic furnishes a curious and interesting study for the Freemason (*Encyclopedia of Freemasonry,* pg. 459).

This would seem odd at first glance; however, it is well known among those who have studied the occult that Freemasonry has many ties to witchcraft and magic. Many Masons study magic, perform magic, enchant, and even possess the ability to fluently speak backwards, all of which are evidences of a foreign or "familiar spirit" (2 Kings 21:6).

The Greek word for "wise" in Matthew 2:1 is *magos*, which is *magian*, that is, an Oriental scientist. The term "magi" only implies magic, but the casting of spells and the working of enchantments were foreign to these Magian travelers. The term "magi" is used for the hereditary priests among the Medes and the Persians. During the time of the Babylonian captivity, there was a Magian group called the Chaldeans, who were considered wise because of their deduction of astral anomalies or astronomy (which of course is different from astrology). The magi of Matthew 2:1 are presumed to be descendants of those Magians or Chaldeans who followed the influence of Daniel the prophet and knew of the coming "Star out of Jacob" (Numbers 24:17). These descendants were continually watching the heavens for signs. The star supplied the evidence they were looking for.

The skills of the magi included philosophy, science and medicine. They were emissaries from one or more of the foreign nations and were seeking the truth. Note also that the star they saw was in the western, not eastern, sky. These wise men lived east of the Holy Land (Matthew 2:1,9). If the star appeared in the eastern sky, the wise men, who lived in the Persian area, would have traveled toward China. Living east of the Holy Land, they saw the star (while they were in the east) in the western sky; therefore, they traveled westward in the general direction of the star! (See *The Joy of Christmas,* a publication of Royal Oak Assembly, Elizabethtown, KY). Most biblical expositors agree that the magi came from the east.

There would be a problem if they followed this star. Noting that their trip took nearly two years (Matthew 2:7,16), they: went to the wrong city (Jerusalem); went to the wrong building (the palace); and talked with the wrong man (King Herod). Matthew 2:7-8 states that the king sent the wise men to Bethlehem. They didn't go there because they were following a star, but because they were instructed to do so by Herod. However, as they departed Jerusalem (v.9), they "looked" heavenward and the "star" reappeared (v.10), giving them cause to rejoice.

The Five-Pointed Star

The star symbol of the Eastern Star is quite different from the "Star out of Jacob," which represents both King David and King Jesus (Numbers 24:17). The symbol for the Eastern Star is an inverted five-pointed star, that is, it has two points upward and one point downward (Lodges in some states do not use the inverted star). This symbol is more than just an artist's depiction of a star. The five-pointed star is an important symbol in western magic as well as in the Eastern Star. In the *Dictionary of Mysticism and the Occult,* we read:

A five-pointed star. The pentagram is an important symbol in Western magic and represents the four elements surmounted by the Spirit. It is regarded as a symbol of human spiritual inspirations when the point faces upwards; but is a symbol of bestiality and retrograde evolution when facing down (pg. 208).

The inverted five-pointed star is used in witchcraft to represent Baphomet, the demonic goat deity, the same Baphomet of Masonry (remember the goat on the church steeple?). It has two points that extend upward, which hold the horns, two points to the side and down, which hold the ears, and one point downward, which holds the chin and beard.

Why then does the Eastern Star use an inverted five-pointed star if it is in no way associated with Christ?

Occultists, New-Agers, Satanists, magicians, witches and Eastern Star members all use the five-pointed star, which is used to invoke evil spirits. Now imagine the women in your church who are members of the Eastern Star. We are instructed in Scripture to remove ourselves from the very appearance of evil, yet the symbol they use is that of an evil world: "Abstain from all appearance of evil" (1 Thessalonians. 5:22).

Whether white or black, magic is magic and has nothing whatsoever to do with Christianity. Why then does the Eastern Star use an inverted five-pointed star if it is in no way associated with Christ?

The fact is, if the root is corrupt so will be the tree. Freemasonry, the root of the Eastern Star, is corrupt and cannot produce anything but corruption. We have seen that the tenets of Freemasonry are anti-Christian, so what would convince us that the Eastern Star, an adopted form of Masonry, would be any different? Nothing. All evidence reveals the evil associations of the Eastern Star.

The superiority of Masonry has brought Eastern Star adherents into the same spiritual bondage with which they are bound. Moreover, there are Masonic Orders for young boys called DeMolay; for young girls there are groups like Job's Daughters and Rainbow Girls. Boys between the ages of 14 and 21 may join the DeMolay Order, which was named after the crusader Jacques DeMolay. These young men don Dracula-type garb in their meetings and progress through degrees commemorating the death of their namesake, who was burned at the stake. Like the Rainbow Girls and Job's Daughters, the DeMolay Order paves the way to adult versions of paganism. For men and women to encourage their own children to join in their paganism is to bring their children into bondage and under judgment. Psalm 89:30-32 reads, "If his [or her] children forsake my law, and walk not in my judgments; If they break my statutes, and keep not my commandments; Then will I visit their transgression with the rod, and their iniquity with stripes."

It is only natural for those who are blindly enslaved to

cast a snare upon the innocent. Jesus Christ offers freedom from bondage: "If the Son therefore shall make you free, ye shall be free indeed" (John 8:36).

CHAPTER
9

THE SUPERIORITY OF FREEMASONRY

We have learned in this study that members of the Masonic Lodge consider Freemasonry superior to all other spiritual or governmental entities. Its spiritual ties run deeper than those of any other mainline religion. Not only does the Masonic Lodge claim superiority over the female Eastern Star Lodges but also over born-again believers in Christ, who make up the Church. Moreover, any individual or entity outside of the Lodge, other than those endorsed by the Grand Lodge of Freemasonry, is considered profane and unlearned, which includes the Christian. Under the subheading "profane" in the *Encyclopedia of Freemasonry*, we read:

> Hence the original and inoffensive signification of profane is that of being uninitiated; and it is in this sense that it is used in Masonry, simply to designate one who has not been initiated as a Mason (pg. 590).

We learned in Chapter Three that the person who seeks initiation into the Lodge must admit he is "in darkness, and now seeks to be brought to light, and to receive a part in the rights and benefits of this Worshipful Lodge, erected to God and dedicated to the Saints John, as all brothers and fellows have done before" (*Ronayne's Handbook of Freemasonry*, pg 57). Of course, this also applies to the minister of the Gospel and any other born-again Christian.

Common sense says that there is a problem when Pastor John is seeking light, that Jesus, according to Masonry, is not a Light sufficient enough to dispel darkness and that the church from which he comes is inferior to the "Worshipful Lodge" that was "erected to God." As we have already mentioned, the god of Freemasonry is not the God of the Bible. *Webster's Dictionary* sheds some light in its definition of the word "profane": 1) characterized by irreverence for God or sacred things; 2) not devoted to religious purposes; secular; 3) unholy; heathen; pagan: profane rites; 4) not initiated into religious rites or mysteries.

> *Freemasonry recognizes no particular redeemer, yet places an emphasis on God, who is considered "above all the Baalim."*

Again we see a role reversal that glorifies the bad and defames the good. A "regular" or "well-governed" Lodge claims superiority over Lodges that include the name of Jesus in their prayers and ceremonies. Freemasonry recognizes no particular redeemer, yet places an emphasis on God, who, as we have seen, is considered "above all the Baalim." Again, this places Jesus in the category of "all the Baalim." Lodges that do recognize Jesus are deemed "irregular" or "clandestine" (subversive, deceptive). To demote Christ in this manner is unquestionably anti-Christian. Masons usually conclude their prayers with phrases such as "in your name." But the Apostle Paul was very specific in his letter instructing the Colossians in the way that they should close their prayers: "And whatsoever ye do in word or deed, do all in the name of the Lord Jesus, giving thanks to God and the Father by him" (Colossians 3:17).

Prince Hall Lodges and the Ku Klux Klan

A "regular" or "well-governed" Lodge claims superiority over Lodges that do not fit their description of legality, or, more specifically, those of other races. These are also considered clandestine Lodges. (This is like the fox guarding the chickens.) One such clandestine Lodge is called the Prince Hall Grand Lodge for Blacks, and includes all Lodges that branch out from it. Under the subheading "Negro Lodges" in the *Encyclopedia of Freemasonry*, we read:

> Admitting even the legality of the English Charter of 1784 — it will be seen that there was already a Masonic authority in Massachusetts upon whose prerogatives of jurisdiction such Charter was an invasion — it cannot be denied that the unrecognized self-revival of 1827, and the subsequent assumption of Grand Lodge powers, were illegal, and rendered both the Prince Hall Grand Lodge and all the Lodges which emanated from it clandestine. And this has been the unanimous opinion of all Masonic jurists in America (pg. 508).

Moreover, racism abounds within the Masonic ranks. *From Christianity and American Freemasonry* by William J. Whalen, revised by *Our Sunday Visitor,* we read:

> An organization dedicated to brotherhood, Masonry ironically remains a bulwark of racial segregation in the United States. By 1987, decades after

most American institutions had accepted racial integration, only four of the forty-nine Grand Lodges could count even one black member in their jurisdictions. As the author of a recent scholarly study of black Freemasonry observes, 'The legitimization of social intermingling between black and white Masons has remained anathema in mainstream Freemasonry (*Our Sunday Visitor*, 1987, pgs. 23–25).

Multiple sources report that Ku Klux Klan membership is almost exclusively obtained through Masonic membership. In *Freemasonry Watch, Freemasonry's History of Racism*, we read:

> Klan and Black Legion meetings were usually held inside Masonic temples and halls in the Midwest during the 1930's. The Klan recruited almost exclusively from within Masonic ranks and often the membership of both organizations was indistinguishable. All of the leadership of the old and new Klan was high degree Freemasons. The Ku Klux Klan was in fact a Masonic movement (For more info, see www.freemasonrywatch.org/racisim.html).

This statement should cause great embarrassment to Masons who profess Christianity. Many indisputable evidences

...black or white, Freemasonry is still unmitigated paganism.

document Albert Pike's heavy involvement in the KKK. Of course, that doesn't excuse African-American members of the Masonic Lodge because black or white, Freemasonry is still unmitigated paganism. Even today the superiority of Caucasian Masons over African-American Masons remains strong.

Any orderly organization has different positions of leadership. Church government includes pastors, bishops, elders, deacons, and so on; however, there mustn't be any type of racial discrimination within the confines of a particular organization or church. All workings should be straightforward and fall within the guidelines of the Word of Truth. The Truth is found only in Jesus Christ. In fact, church leaders are expected to be servants and not dictators of the congregations. In addition, Christians are instructed to teach "all" nations, not just certain nations and people (Matthew 28:19).

Spiritual Bondage

Whether they know it or not, Lodge members and their families are either directly or indirectly involved with ancient paganism, cults, racist groups, hate mongers and infidels, all of which oppose Christ's teachings of love for our fellow man and salvation through Him alone. We have clearly seen that Freemasonry places a great emphasis on good works, even to the extent that they are necessary for gaining entrance into the "Celestial Lodge above." This cannot be true in any sense of the word; Freemasonry is corrupt and has corrupted millions, ensnaring them in spiritual bondage. The Apostle Peter wrote about such bondage in his second letter: "While they promise them liberty, they themselves are the servants of corruption: for of whom a man is overcome, of the same is he brought in bondage" (2 Peter 2:19).

The bondage of Freemasonry has affected the spiritual course of many individuals — even entire denominations — supplying the means by which many people sentence themselves to hell by trusting in the wrong things for admittance into the kingdom of God. Spiritual bondage equals spiritual blindness.

Freemasonry is corrupt and has corrupted millions, ensnaring them in spiritual bondage.

This is why it is so difficult to reach men and women involved with the Lodge. Members of Masonry are mirrors of those people who lived during Isaiah's day: "They have not known nor understood: for he hath shut their eyes, that they cannot see; and their hearts, that they cannot understand" (Isaiah 44:18).

Many individuals cannot even see the resemblance of evil simply because they possess the wrong spirit. Such people are spiritually blind to the Truth. God does not tolerate such wickedness nor will He reside in an unclean heart. All have sinned and must accept Christ and His plan for eternal life if they are to be truly healed of their spiritual blindness and brought to Jesus, who is the only source of true Light.

"Then spake Jesus again unto them, saying I am the light of the world: he that followeth me shall not walk in darkness, but shall have the light of life" (John 8:12).

The only way to know this truth is to read the Bible and believe that what it says is in fact God-breathed and absolutely true or else you will remain in darkness: "But the natural man receiveth not the things of the Spirit of God: for they are foolishness unto him: neither can he know them, because they are spiritually discerned. But he that is spiritual judgeth all things, yet he himself is judged of no man. For who hath known the mind of the Lord, that he may instruct him? But we have the mind of Christ" (1 Corinthians 2:14–16).

Christian Impact

If someone truly cares about you they will tell you the truth in love. Christians are to lovingly reveal the truth. We cannot save anyone, but our obligation as believers is to proclaim the Gospel of Jesus Christ. Scripture promises that those who are set free from their bondage are free indeed (John 8:36).

We cannot save anyone, but our obligation as believers is to proclaim the Gospel of Jesus Christ.

Change always comes about when the truth is spoken in love. Many Christian outreaches to Masons and efforts to reveal the conflict between Masonry and Christianity have not been in vain. Many have realized the contradictions, have renounced the cult

112

of Freemasonry and have withdrawn their membership from the Lodge. At present, an estimated 70 percent of all Masons are inactive. The pace of Lodge membership is now in decline, due in part to age. In 1990, 40 percent of all Masons were over the age of 65.

Recent attempts have been made to revitalize the organization's dwindling membership. What used to take three months to obtain 29 degrees of the Scottish rite may now be obtained in a single weekend. This also reveals Masonry's shift in principle when the need arises. Some states have reduced to a single day the initiation time for obtaining a Master Mason degree. Furthermore, the Shrine Club now accepts Third-degree Masons straight from the Blue Lodge. In previous years, only 32nd–degree Masons were allowed to become members of the Shrine Club (*The Good Word*, by Tom McKenney, Dec.2002; Jan. 2003).

At present, an estimated 70 percent of all Masons are inactive.

A significant number of Masons still hold governing positions in churches across our nation. As a result, many Christian churches continue to decline in membership and strife within churches continues. Many churches survive the pressures of Masonic spiritualism, but most lack the leading of the Holy Spirit. This is not due to a lack of power on the part of the

Holy Spirit, but to God's lack of tolerance for ungodly principles. God expects His people to be holy and set apart. It must be noted that these "good men made better" may have the best of intentions and may truly care about their churches; however, Masonic involvement in paganism has promoted a spiritless form of worship, which is suffocating—or better yet, stagnating—the work of the Holy Spirit. In essence, it's the blind leading the blind (Matthew 15:14).

Many Masons have the ability to quote Scripture and recite Bible stories verbatim but that ability isn't what makes people Christians. Salvation and eternal life are not found in good works, emotion or even sincerity. This is

Salvation and eternal life are not found in good works, emotion or even sincerity.

where it becomes difficult for many to discern their spiritual condition. There are many who "profess" but who do not "possess." "But strong meat belongeth to them that are of full age, even those who by reason of use have their senses exercised to discern both good and evil" (Hebrews 5:14).

Many of the men and women who are dedicated to the Lodge are no doubt spiritual people, but they possess the wrong spirit. We may criticize their church and receive little to no reaction, but look out if we make the same comments about their Lodge. Why? Because an evil spirit is lurking and it does not wish to be disturbed. We must reach out to those who are involved in the deceptive practices of the Masonic Lodge with a loving, caring, and compassionate attitude. In 1 Corinthians 13:8, the Apostle Paul explains that love never fails. Prayer is also an essential ingredient in reaching out to Masons. They may become angry because of our witness, but positive fruit will be produced either immediately or at some point down the road if they truly wish to do what is right before God. James 1:5 says that if we pray for wisdom we will receive it.

The Apostle Paul addressed those who are involved in Masonry, Adoptive Masonry, or one of Masonry's many branches in the following passage:

> Be ye not unequally yoked together with unbelievers: for what fellowship hath righteousness with unrighteousness: and what communion hath light with darkness? And what concord hath Christ with Belial? Or what part hath he that believeth with an infidel? And what agreement hath the temple of God with idols? For ye are the temple of the living God; as God hath said, I will dwell in them, and walk in them; and I will be their God, and they shall be my people. Wherefore come out from among them, and be ye separate, saith the Lord, and touch not the unclean thing; and I will receive you. And will be a Father unto you, and ye shall be my sons and daughters, saith the Lord Almighty (2 Corinthians 6:14–18).

CHAPTER
1 0

COME NOW, LET US
REASON TOGETHER

Reason is the ability to determine or to conclude by logical thinking. In Isaiah 1:18 the Lord said: "Come now, and let us reason together." The resolution to the conflict between Masonry and Christianity boils down to this: Either Christianity is true or it isn't. This is not merely a difference of opinion; the contradictions between the two organizations' principles demand that only one can be right.

Freemasonry Doctrine: Is It Reasonable?

It becomes undeniably clear, according to the evidence that Freemasonry cannot stand. The Bible says, "no good thing will he [God] withhold from them that walk uprightly" (Psalm 84:11). But the Christian who is not a Mason *does* have good things withheld from him if Freemason principles are true. Further, if those principles are true, then a great injustice has been committed in its practice of "ever concealing and never revealing" because Ephesians 5:13 says "whatsoever doth make manifest is light."

The resolution to the conflict between Masonry and Christianity boils down to this: Either Christianity is true or it isn't.

If the doctrine of Freemasonry is "true" as Masonic authorities insist, then recipients of the Holy Ghost on the Day of Pentecost must have been a group of overly emotional individuals and the disciples must have been persecuted for spreading only a "likeness" of the truth. This would make Jesus guilty of persuading untold numbers to follow Him, and His true followers would have settled for less than the "complete" truth. If the foundation of Freemasonry is true, then millions of people have given their lives for a lie.

Moses a Mason: Is It Reasonable?

Since Christianity *is* true, Freemasonry is counterfeit, especially considering that the Blue Degrees (first three) are "intentionally misled by false interpretation" (*Morals and Dogma*, pg. 819).

Masonry teaches that Moses, Paul and others were initiates of the mystery religions of Freemasonry. If Christianity is true, then isn't it reasonable to think that although Moses was "learned in all the wisdom of the Egyptians" (Acts 7:22) that he separated himself, and later his people, from the ways of the Egyptians? (See Chapter Five).

Is it reasonable to assume that although Saul (Paul) was schooled in the Kabbala (*Morals and Dogma*, pg. 769; see also "Kabbala" – Appendix A), he found the true Light (Jesus) on the road to Damascus and later wrote about the "mystery of iniquity" (2 Thessalonians 2:7)? The word "mystery" comes from the Greek word *musterion,* meaning "a secret, or mystery (through the idea of silence imposed by initiation into religious rites" (*Strong's Concordance of the Bible*). "Iniquity" or anomia [Greek]—is the "wickedness or unrighteousness" of 2 Thessalonians 2:7.

Egyptian Legend: Is It Reasonable?

We tend to think of Egyptian legend as part of the ancient past; however, its philosophy has far exceeded the realm of history. Its presence has survived not only through Freemasonry, but also from the deep infusion in the continued teaching of great philosophers who themselves were seekers of light. The Egyptian mysteries abundantly supplied these men with such ability to altar the conscience of mankind. *The General History of Freemasonry* by Emmanuel Rebold and J. F. Brennan contains evidence of the common object of the mysteries and how they relate to us:

Is it reasonable that this religious brotherhood would embrace all redeemers without any focus on Jesus Christ?

> Thus we see the most illustrious men of Greece – Thales, Solon, Pythagoras, Democritus, Orpheus, Plato, Theldosius, Epicurus, Herodotus, Lycurgus – these great philosophers of antiquity, binding their stoutest sandals upon their feet, and taking the pilgrim's staff within their hands, leaving their country and going forth to visit the vast sanctuaries of Egypt, they're to be initiated into the mysteries of Isis and Osiris *(A General History of Freemasonry*, J.F. Brennan, Publisher, 1885, pg. 31).

Is it reasonable to assume that these great philosophers who made their mark on the world through Egyptian legend contributed in planting the seeds of a utopian one-worldedness, only to have them grow in a society anxious to grab at a New World Order? Is it reasonable that this religious brotherhood would embrace all redeemers without any focus on Jesus Christ? I think so!

> Masonry, not in anywise derogating from the differing duties which the diversity of states requires, tends to create a new people, which composed of men of many nations and tongues, shall all be bound together by the bonds of science, morality and virtue (*Morals and Dogma*, pg. 220).

More Than One Way: Is It Reasonable?

God does not and man cannot force anyone to believe or reject any truth. The choice is left up to the individual. The following quotes from Masonic sources and the Bible are for your evaluation, as is the entirety of this work; so come now, let us reason together.

"We do not undervalue the importance of any Truth. We utter no word that can be deemed irreverent by any one of any faith. "We do not tell the Muslim that it is only important for him to believe that there is but one God, and wholly unessential whether Mohammed was His prophet. We do not tell the Hebrew that the Messiah whom he expects was born in Bethlehem nearly two thousand years ago; and that he is a heretic because he will not so believe. And little do we tell the Christian that Jesus of Nazareth was but a man like us, or His history but the unreal revival of an older legend. To do either is beyond our jurisdiction. Masonry, of no one age, belongs to all time; of no one religion, it finds its great truths in all" (*Morals and Dogma*, pg. 524).

The Apostle Peter wrote: "But there were false prophets also among the people, even as there shall be false teachers among you, who privily shall bring in damnable heresies, even denying the Lord that bought them, and bring upon themselves swift destruction. And many shall follow their pernicious ways; by reason of whom the way of truth shall be evil spoken of" (2 Peter 2:1–2).

"The Teachers, even of Christianity, are, in general, the most ignorant of the true meaning of that which they teach" (*Morals and Dogma*, pg. 105).

In his first letter to the Corinthians, the Apostle Paul wrote: "But the natural man receiveth not the things of the Spirit of God: for they are foolishness unto him: neither can he know them, because they are spiritually discerned" (1 Corinthians 2:14).

"Every Mason must keep his lawful secrets, and aid him in his business, defend his character, when unjustly assailed, and protect, counsel, and assist his widow and his orphans" (*Morals and Dogma*, pg. 726).

"And through covetousness shall they with feigned words make merchandise of you: whose judgment now of a long time lingereth not, and their damnation slumbereth not" (2 Peter 2:3).

"The Blue Degrees are but the outer court or portico of the Temple. Part of the symbols are displayed there to the initiate, but he is intentionally misled by false interpretations" (*Morals and Dogma*, pg. 819).

"For there are certain men crept in unawares, who were before of old ordained to this condemnation, ungodly men, turning the grace of our God into lasciviousness, and denying the only Lord God, and our Lord Jesus Christ" (Jude 1:4).

"There is no book of which so little is known as the Bible. To most who read it, it is as incomprehensible as the Sohar" (*Morals and Dogma*, pg. 105).

"But these, as natural brute beasts, made to be taken and destroyed, speak evil of the things that they understand not; and shall utterly perish in their own corruption" (2 Peter 2:12).

"He improves his moral nature, becomes a better man, and finds in the reunion of virtuous men, assembled with pure views, the means of multiplying his acts of beneficence" (*Morals and Dogma*, pg. 325).

"Spots they are and blemishes, sporting themselves with their own deceivings while they feast with you. Having eyes full of adultery, and that cannot cease from sin; beguiling unstable souls: an heart they have exercised with covetous practices; cursed children" (2 Peter 2:13–14).

Masonry propagates no creed except its own most simple and sublime one; that universal religion, taught by nature and by reason. Its Lodges are neither Jewish, Muslim, nor Christian temples. It reiterates the precepts of morality of all religions. It venerates the character and commends the teachings of the great and good of all ages and of all countries. It extracts the good and not the evil, the truth, and not the error, from all creeds; and acknowledges that there is much which is good and true in all (*Morals and Dogma*, pg. 718).

"These are wells without water, clouds that are carried with a tempest to whom the mist of darkness is reserved for ever. For when they speak great swelling words of vanity, they allure through the lusts of the flesh, through much wantonness, those that were clean escaped from them who live in error" (2 Peter 2:17–18).

To sow, that others may reap; to work and plant for those who are to occupy the earth when we are dead; to project our influences far into the future, and live beyond our time; to rule as the Kings of Thought, over men who are yet unborn; to bless with the glorious gifts of truth and light and liberty those who will neither know the name of the giver, nor care in what grave his unregarded ashes repose, is the true office of a Mason and the proudest destiny of man (*Morals and Dogma*, pg. 317).

"While they promise them liberty, they themselves are the servants of corruption: for of whom a man is overcome, of the same is he brought in bondage" (2 Peter 2:19).

The "Light" of Masonry: Is It Reasonable?

Masonry is a search for light, but there is no proof that the "light" is ever truly attained. In fact, the

Masons teach that light can never be found. But the one who receives Christ Jesus does receive "Light," for Jesus is the Light. Although much is to be learned and accomplished by the new Christian, he or she has been given the "Light" through which those things may be obtained.

As we see many church members becoming involved with and joining the Lodge, is it reasonable to assume that the dissension of the Church today is because of Baal worship as in the Old Testament? It appears so.

Such worship in the Old Testament brought ruin upon God's people as well as the entire nation. This worship also caused the dead-

...the one who receives Christ Jesus does receive "Light," for Jesus is the Light.

ening of the conscience, which resulted in intermarriage with pagans, sodomy and child sacrifice. Today the percentage of divorce and remarriage are alarming; sodomy remains rampant and 1.5 million babies are aborted annually. And we dare call ourselves a Christian nation?

The results of unrighteousness are not due to having good men in the Lodge, but that these good men are being duped into worshipping Baal under the pretense that it is the one true God. According to Scripture, the Mason who claims to be a Christian is actually serving two masters. The Bible teaches that this will not work (Luke 16:12–13). Christians are to set the standard (Romans 3:31).

If a man desires to be a Mason, so be it, but he must separate himself from the church. D.L. Moody said, "A man who would rather leave the church than leave the Lodge can't leave the church too soon." If a man desires to be a Christian and worship according to biblical

> "A man who would rather leave the church than leave the Lodge can't leave the church too soon"
> –D.L. Moody

principles, then let him separate himself from the Lodge. If a man desires a life of contradiction and deceit, a life to be pitied, let him try and be both (James 1:8).

Thank God for those individuals who have recognized the conflict in principles and have separated themselves from the Lodge, and have come to Christ and recognized Him as "Lord."

"Then said Jesus to those Jews which believed on him, If ye continue in my word, then are ye my disciples indeed; And ye shall know the truth, and the truth shall make you free" (John 8:31–32).

If you are a Lodge member and a church member and have never known that there are doctrinal contradictions between Masonry and Christianity and have read this far, then you are now without excuse. I urge you to give yourself totally to Christ. The Bible says that all have sinned (Romans 3:23); that there is eternal life only through Jesus Christ (John 3:16); that to reject Jesus is to continue in sin and receive its wages, which is death (Romans 6:23); and that if you confess Jesus as Lord and believe in His resurrection you will be saved (Romans 10:9). If you have never been born again of the Spirit, then ask the Lord Jesus to save you. Then be baptized and "walk worthy of the vocation wherewith ye are called" (Ephesians 4:1).

APPENDIX A

KABBALA

Entire volumes have been written on the Kabbala without nearly exhausting its content or its depth because it is not a particular document or book but is an oral tradition of a secret wisdom. In these few pages I will only focus on the most outstanding points of Kabbalistic knowledge.

The word "Kabbala" (also spelled with a Q, C, and other variations) is derived from the Hebrew word *kabal,* meaning, "to receive." It is the doctrine received from the "elders," a mystical philosophy or theosophy, a science of Jewish rabbis, to interpret the hidden meaning of the first five books of the Old Testament known as the Pentateuch. The Kabbala, however, is occultic knowledge.

Mackey writes this about the role the Kabbala plays in Masonry in his book, *Encyclopedia of Freemasonry:* "Much use is made of it in the high degrees, and entire Rites have been constructed on its principles" (pg. 375).

The tradition of the Kabbala is presumed to have come from God and been communicated to a select company of angels. These angels passed it to Adam, and it eventually spread to Noah and Abraham, who immigrated with it to Egypt. Aided by an angel, Moses presumably devoted his leisure to the study of the Kabbala during his 40 years of wandering in the wilderness. Thus, he concealed the principles of this secret doctrine in the Pentateuch. Jewish scholars hold to this theory.

The Kabbala is divided into two classes: Practical

and Theoretical. The practical Kabbala is used in instructions for the construction of talisman and amulets and has no direct connection with Masonic science. Masonic science however, is endued with the theoretical Kabbala, which is again divided into two groups: Dogmatic and Literal.

The most common method of interpretation is through *gematria*, (i.e., transposing Hebrew words and phrases into numerical equivalents). Words and phrases with the same numeric value are believed to be related. Other methods include *notaricon* and *temura*, although they have variations, they have similar qualities to *gematria*. These are divisions of the Literal Kabbala.

It is presumed that Dogmatic Kabbala was derived from Zoroaster, a 6th-century B.C. Persian religious teacher. Zoroaster believed in one God: Ahura Mazda. From Ahura Mazda or the *En Soph* ("infinite one") were 10 emanations or *hephiroth* (intelligences) through which he created all that is:

- *kether* – the crown
- *chokma* – wisdom
- *binah* – understanding
- *chesed* – mercy
- *geburah* – power
- *taphareth* – beauty and harmony
- *netzach* – victory
- *hod* – splendor or glory
- *yeshod* – foundation
- *malkuth* – the kingdom

The Kabbala is first, a theory of these emanations. The 10 emanations listed in three columns represent three pillars of the Kabbalistic Tree of Life. The left pillar consists of understanding, power or strength, splendor or glory. The middle pillar is composed of the crown, beauty and harmony, the foundation, and the kingdom. The right pillar is wisdom, mercy, and victory. The right and left-hand pillars in Masonry represent those pillars of Solomon's temple.

In relation to these pillars of the Kabbalistic Tree, Pike relates: "Victory is YAHOVAH-TSABAOTH, the column on the right hand, the column Jachin: Glory is the column Boaz, on the left hand. And thus our symbols appear again in the Kabbala" (*Morals and Dogma,* pg. 267).

Occultists use the Kabbalistic Tree of Life as a matrix or grid for comparing the archetypal images of different mythologies that could be adapted to ceremonial magic. For example, the merciful father (*chesed*) has parallels in other pantheons; namely Odin (Scandinavia), Zeus (Greece), Jupiter (Rome), and Ra (Egypt). This system of comparison became known as mythological correspondences. It has also become common in the occult tradition to link the 10 *sephiroth* of the Tree of Life with the 22 cards of the Major Arcana of the Tarot, a link first proposed by the magician Eliphas Levi (*Dictionary of Mysticism and the Occult*).

"All truly dogmatic religions have issued from the Kabbala and return to it: everything scientific and grand in the religious dreams of all the illuminati, Jacob Boehme, Swedenborg, Saint Martin, and others, is borrowed from the Kabbala; all the Masonic associations owe to it their Secrets and their Symbols" (*Morals and Dogma*, pg. 744).

In keeping with the occultic sciences, Freemasonry's universality is thus in parallel, that is, reverencing all reformers or redeemers: "This is precisely the creed of the old Buddhists of Samaneans, who believed that from time to time God sent Buddhas on earth, to reform men, to wean them from their vices, and lead them back into the paths of virtue" (*Morals and Dogma*, pg. 365).

"The first Masonic Legislator whose memory is preserved to us by history, was Buddha, who, about a thousand years before the Christian era, reformed the religion of Manous. He called to the Priesthood all men, without distinction of caste, who felt themselves inspired by God to instruct men" (*Morals and Dogma*, pg. 277).

Considering all the precepts of the Kabbala and its instruction in talisman, magic, and pantheistic lore, it leaves little wonder why Christ rebuked the scribes and the Pharisees for placing more emphasis on tradition than the written law (Matthew 15:1-6; Mark 7:3-13; see also 1 Peter 1:18).

In addition, as the Kabbala is a mystical Jewish philosophy, Paul warned Titus, "Not giving heed to Jewish fables, and commandments of men, that turn from the truth" (Titus 1:14).

"Beware lest any man spoil you through philosophy and vain deceit, after the tradition of men, after the rudiments of the world, and not after Christ. For in him dwelleth all the fullness of the Godhead [divinity] bodily" (Colossians 2:8-9).

Christianity is not a mystical search nor in the keeping of the Law per se, for the Law was but a foreshadow of Christ (Hebrews 10:1); Christ fulfilled the Law (Matthew 5:17) ("fulfill" — "to make replete, abundantly filled").

"Think not that I [Jesus] am come to destroy the law, or the prophets: I am not come to destroy, but to fulfil" (Matthew 5:17).

The Law then, is not our labor but our instructor.

"Wherefore the law was our schoolmaster to bring us unto Christ, that we might be justified by faith. But after that faith is come, we are no longer under a schoolmaster. For ye are all the children of God by faith in Christ Jesus" (Galatians 3:24–26).

APPENDIX B
SPURIOUS
FREEMASONRY

The connections to the mysteries in Chapter Five of this book (Masonic Roots) should not be unfamiliar to a well-read Mason, as they are aware that such "roots" exist. There must, however, be another interpretation that is not offensive to Christians and other sectarian faiths; thus, the development of "Spurious" Freemasonry.

"Spurious Masonry" or "False Masonry" is set apart from "irregular" or "clandestine" Lodges. An "irregular" Lodge is a legally created Lodge that continues to operate even after its Charter has been revoked. Additionally, Lodges considered irregular are those that do not conform to the established rule. A "clandestine" Lodge operates without the consent of a Grand Lodge. Masons consider Chapter Five of this book as being "Spurious" or "False." This deserves a response.

Spurious Masonry is the supposed parallel of the "true" or "primitive" system and sprang from a corrupt lineage. According to Masonry, Seth, Adam's son, and his descendants preserved the true principles of Masonry, while the rebellious Cain and his descendants maintained a false or Spurious Masonry.

Encyclopedia of Freemasonry defines Spurious Masonry in the following way:

> The descendants of Seth, becoming corrupted by their frequent communications with those of Cain, adopted their manners, and soon lost the principles of the primitive Freemasonry, which at length were confined to Noah and his three sons, who alone, in the

destruction of a wicked world, were thought worthy
of receiving mercy (pg. 707).

Here Mackey expounds upon the theory of Dr.
George Oliver, an English Mason who contended for
the Christian character of the Lodge. A better descrip-
tion of Oliver's theory is found under the heading
"Primitive Freemasonry" in *Encyclopedia of
Freemasonry*:

> The primitive Freemasonry of the antediluvians is
> a term which we are indebted to Oliver, although the
> theory was broached by earlier writers, and among
> them by the Chevalier Ramsey. The theory is, that the
> principles of Freemasonry existed in the earliest ages
> of the world, and were believed and practiced by a
> primitive people, or priesthood, under the name of
> pure or primitive Freemasonry; and that this
> Freemasonry, that is to say, the religious doctrine
> inculcated by it, was, after the flood, corrupted by the
> pagan philosophers and priests, and receiving the title
> of "Spurious Freemasonry," was exhibited in the
> Ancient Mysteries. The Noachide, however, preserved
> the principles of the primitive Freemasonry, and trans-
> mitted them to succeeding ages, when at length they
> assumed the name of "Speculative Masonry." The
> primitive Freemasonry was probably without ritual or
> symbolism, and consisted only of a series of abstract
> propositions derived from antediluvian traditions. Its
> dogmas were the unity of God and the immortality of
> the soul (pg. 584).

In accordance with Oliver's theory, Ham, Noah's
son — being familiar with the system of Cain —

revived all the corruptions of Spurious Freemasonry after the Flood. Hence, two systems of Masonry again thrived: one that was through Adam, Enoch, and Noah and the other was through the lineage of Cain, adopted by Ham. It is apparent that this theory was created for the benefit of its Christian members. Mackey confirms that "the theory is an attractive one. But if we attempt to contend that there was among the patriarchs any esoteric organization at all resembling the modern system of Freemasonry, we shall find no historical date on which we may rely for support" (*Encyclopedia of Freemasonry,* pg. 584).

Mackey also cites the sources from which Oliver drew his conclusions as being "sketchy" or crude. We read:

> The great error of Dr. Oliver, as a Masonic teacher, was a too easy credulity or a too great warmth of imagination, which led him to accept without hesitation the crude theories of previous writers, and to recognize documents and legends as unquestionably authentic whose truthfulness subsequent researches have led most Masonic scholars to doubt or to deny. His statements, therefore, as to the history of the Order, have to be received with many grains of allowance. Yet it must be acknowledged that no writer in the English language has ever done so much to elevate the scientific character of Freemasonry (pg. 529).

If Oliver's theory concerning Spurious Freemasonry were true, wouldn't it seem illogical to know that a true Masonry exists yet to continue to practice the doctrines of a "corrupted" Masonry?

The diligent study of any subject demands evidence for truth rather than speculation. Since there is no historical support for the theory of Spurious Freemasonry being attributed to the Ancient Mysteries, the answer becomes obvious, especially when the evidence is considered. Freemasonry is a continuation of the Ancient Mysteries as stated by Masonic authorities and confirmed by history.

Modern Freemasonry and the Ancient Mystery religions are more historically and biblically substantiated as being of common origin.

APPENDIX C

THE TRINITY OF BAALIM

We discussed the philosophical roots of Freemasonry in Chapter Five and honed in on Nimrod, the son of Cush, from the lineage of Ham as being the key figure. In this chapter we will focus on the deluded religion associated with goddesses and with the great god Baal (Nimrod). The information in Chapter Five will serve as a springboard for our exploration of the trinity of Baalim.

One of the doctrinal pillars of Christianity is the "threefold personality of the one-divine God" (1 John 5:7) but many are unaware of the existence of a false trinity. This trinity consists of Satan (anti-God), the Antichrist or "man of sin" (anti-Son), and the False Prophet (anti-Spirit).

This mock trinity will be revealed in the latter days during the Tribulation Period, a structured one-world government and religious system presently being formed. This trinity was also represented at the first organized revolt against God after the Flood. We see this triad in Cush, Nimrod, and Semiramis.

After the confusion of languages following the building of the Tower of Babel, Nimrod was later deified under the name Merodach or Baal. Baal is also known as the son of El, the "father of the gods." Although "El" is a name attributed to God, it is a generic name for God in Northwest Semitic (Hebrew and Ugaritic) and as such is also employed in the Old Testament for heathen deities (Exodus 34:14; Psalm 81:10; Isaiah 44:10).

Since Nimrod is Baal, the reference to his father,

El, is Cush. Cush is believed to have been the main instigator of the building of the tower of Babel and of Babylon. The name "Cush" is a Chaldaic form of the word "chaos," which means confusion. This brings to light the intermixed names Bel and Baal of history. Baal signifies "the lord," while Bel means "to confound, or bring to confusion."

Jeremiah wrote, "every founder is confounded" (10:14; 51:17). Thus "chaos" (confusion) or Bel (to confound) must refer to Cush, Nimrod's father. This is disclosed in Jeremiah 50:2, where we read that "Bel is confounded, Merodach is broken in pieces"; that is, the founder is confounded and Merodach is disrupted. This reflects the duality of Bel and Baal (Merodach) as separate entities: father and son.

More Evidence

It was Nimrod, however, of whom it was said, "he began to be mighty upon the earth" (1 Chronicles 1:10). Thus, Baal became synonymous with Bel as founder, for Cush — referred as only the father, and particularly as a god — had faded into obscurity. This alludes to Genesis 10:10, where the "beginning of his kingdom was Babel." That is, the "first" of Nimrod's dominion (from the Hebrew *malak*, "to ascend the throne") was Babel, which implies a city already undergoing formation. Later Nimrod built Erech, Accad, and Calneh and consolidated them into one kingdom under his own rule. This was the first state of imperialism.

During this rise to dominion, Cush had apparently died (or possibly was murdered). His wife, Semiramis, gained control through her son, Nimrod. Nimrod is known historically as the "husband of the mother" because Nimrod married his mother — an apparent continuance of the practice of incestuous relationships, which grandfather Ham had begun (Genesis 9:24). Note: This parallels the Isis and Osiris legend. This mother/son rule was the beginning of goddess worship, to which Israel often fell prey. This goddess is often recognized alongside the respective god: "And they forsook the Lord, and served Baal and Ashtaroth...and served Baalim and Ashtaroth" (Judges 2:13; 10:6). "Then the children of Israel did put away Baalim and Ashtaroth, and served the Lord only" (1 Samuel 7:4; 12:10).

"For Solomon went after Ashtaroth the goddess of the Zidonians, and after Milcom the abomination of the Ammonites" (1 Kings 11:5 — See also 11:33; 2 Kings 23:13).

"Which made silver shrines for Diana...So that not only our craft is in danger to be set a nought; but also that the temple of the great goddess Diana should be destroyed, whom all Asia and the world worshippeth" (Acts 19:24; 19:27; see also 19:28,29).

(Note: Baalim are not images of Baal but various concepts of the "god.") This god and goddess continue to be worshipped today under the guise of the "mother and child"; prayers are offered to the mother as well as to the son. In his book, *Morals and Dogma*, Pike stated:

144

> The God of nineteen-twentieths of the Christian world is only Bel, Moloch, Zeus, or at best Osiris, Mithras, or Adonai, under another name, worshipped with the old pagan ceremonies and ritualistic formulas. It is the statue of Olympian Jove, worshipped as the Father, in the Christian church that was a pagan temple; it is the statue of Venus, become the Virgin Mary (pgs. 295, 296).

(Note: The above quotation is an obvious reference to Catholicism, since the religion is notorious for its expressions of adoration for idols.)

Again we find the mock trinity:

- Cush, displaced by Satan, for Cush faded into obscurity as a god (anti-God)
- Nimrod (anti-Son)
- Semiramis (anti-Spirit), for she instigated observances and laws

In like manner, the confusion of languages provided a variety of names and attributes for this goddess while Bel and Baal eventually became synonymous in title and in attribute.

Was it Murder?

It is believed that Osiris (Nimrod/Baal) murdered his brother Typhon. To get a clear picture of the relationship we must first understand the meaning of the Old Testament term "kinsman," which was used in a variety of ways and could refer to a father, mother, brother, nephew, or other relative. Typhon is believed to be Shem, the "kinsman," or great uncle of

145

Nimrod.

We must remember that Typhon was considered evil. Why? It is a common practice for those who are in error to claim they are "of God" when they are not. It is only natural for the ungodly to accuse those who truly are of God as being of Satan; this is an obvious reversal of roles. In this reversal of roles, Nimrod (Osiris/Baal) was murdered by Shem and was cut into 14 pieces when he was actually trying to rid the people of idolatry. In Chapter Five we learned that Osiris' remains were scattered around the kingdom. The reason for such an act is alluded to in 1 Samuel 11:7. In this example, Saul cut a yoke of oxen in pieces and sent them throughout the coasts of Israel. He said to the people: "Whosoever cometh not forth after Saul and after Samuel, so shall it be done unto his oxen. And the fear of the Lord fell on the people, and they came out with one consent."

Apparently this custom came from the action displayed by Shem. Such an action would strongly express that those who continued the practices of Osiris (Nimrod) would suffer the same fate. This action may have been the cause of the secretive nature of these Ancient Mysteries that Freemasonry succeeds.

APPENDIX D

FREEMASONRY AND THE NEW AGE REVIVAL

The world at large is experiencing a surge of spiritism. Fortune telling, soothsaying, palm reading, séances, tarot card reading, horoscopes, psychics, witchcraft, Satanism, and astrology — to name a few — are all part of a new spiritual awakening.

Although it is an age-old phenomenon, this spiritual revival is known collectively as the New Age Movement. The aforementioned branches are only legs of operation. Many such avenues practice channeling, the altering of the consciousness, out-of-body experiences, and similar spiritual occurrences through a medium or "avatar," which is generally used by occultists and theosophists to denote any divine incarnation (*Dictionary of Mysticism and The Occult*, pg. 22). The fundamental principle of New Age is the belief that all is one. In other words, the same spirit or ideal that dwelt in Buddha, Krishna, Rama, and Jesus also dwells in all. We may arrive at our human potential by reaching deep inside ourselves through meditation and by delving into the spirit avenues. By so doing we become "one" with the universe. These new revelations aid us in the search for true enlightenment or self-awareness.

This "all is one" view denies the deity of Jesus by making Him only one of many avatars or incarnations. The claim is that Jesus became one with the "force" or "impersonal presence" (God) as did Buddha, Krishna, et al. This degradation of Jesus Christ is essentially the same given Him by Lodge teaching. (See Chapter One.)

The New Age Movement is attractive in that it brings together the wisdom of the past through Eastern Mysticism and modern science. Its very nature is that of a movement and not of just one particular philosophy. Its tentacles are far-reaching and appear as harmless pursuits of knowledge while they engulf the very soul.

The aberrations of this New Age Movement can be placed in the biblical category called "familiar spirits." Scripture warns many times about this illusive system. Leviticus 19:31: "Regard not them that have familiar spirits, neither seek after wizards, to be defiled by them: I am the LORD your God."

Deuteronomy 18:10-11: "There shall not be found among you any one that maketh his son or his daughter to pass through the fire, or that useth divination, or an observer of times, or an enchanter, or a witch, or a charmer, or a consulter with familiar spirits, or a wizard, or a necromancer" (See also Leviticus 20:6; Isaiah 8:19; 19:3; Daniel 1:20; 2:2; 2:7; 4:7; Exodus 7:11; 12:22; 8:7; 2 Chronicles 33:6).

A Masonic Connection?

Freemasonry and New Age run parallel in many areas. I received the following response from New Age advocate Tara Center to a question I had asked regarding the connection between New Age philosophy and Freemasonry, to which she responded: "According to the Wisdom teachings, the Masonic Movement is one of the three main channels through which the preparation for the new age is going on. It is a far more occult organization than can be realized, and is intended to be the training school for the coming advanced occultists" (excerpt from a personal letter to

Keith Harris of Omega Publishing, dated 5/19/87).

Not only do we find a New Age connection of today but we also find an age-old connection through what Luke calls the "spirit of divination" found in Acts 16:16: "And it came to pass, as we went to prayer, a certain damsel possessed with a spirit of divination met us, which brought her masters much gain by soothsaying."

Luke reported that this damsel followed the Apostle Paul for several days and had a worthy testimony about Paul and his companions. She said these men were servants of the most high God and were showing the way of salvation, which was obviously the truth. Yet Paul cast out of her the spirit of divination because this spirit was a hindrance even though the truth was present.

What was this "Spirit of Divination"?

Vine's Expository Dictionary of New Testament Words defines "divination" as:

> PUTHON (   ), Eng., python, in Greek mythology was the name of the Pythian serpent or dragon, dwelling in Pytho, at the foot of mount Pamassus, guarding the oracle of Delphi, and slain by Apollo. Thence the name was transferred to Apollo himself. Later the word was applied to diviners or soothsayers, regarded as inspired by Apollo. Since demons are the agents inspiring idolatry, 1 Corinthians 10:20, the young woman of Acts 16:16 was possessed by a demon instigating the cult of Apollo, and thus had 'a spirit of divination.'

This "spirit of divination" was then the "spirit of Apollo," or "Python," as he was also called. Apollo is the

150

Greek name for the Egyptian Osiris or Nimrod. This "spirit of Apollo" the damsel possessed was the same as the "spirit of Nimrod," with only a variation of operation. Thus, it was a kindred spirit with Freemasonry.

Those who are involved with Freemasonry are also possessed with this spirit that utters truth, yet that is not truly compatible with that truth. In turn, the Christian world struggles for revival as many prominent church officers cling to Freemasonry. Note the following:

1) New Age spiritism will rage on for as long as those who profess Christianity are of like spirit with them.

2) We cannot defeat the enemy as long as we remain on his side.

3) For true revival to take place, professing Christians must either sever their ties with the Church or with the Lodge.

Notice of Withdrawal

Lodge #_____

City_____

State_____

Gentlemen,

I am petitioning to withdraw from the institution of Freemasonry. After examining the highest documents and authorities and comparing my findings to Christian principles, I have concluded that the god of Masonry is not the God of the Bible. I find the practices of the Craft are based on and descend from the Ancient Mystery religions. This opposes my Christian convictions. I feel no animosity toward you or to others in affiliation with Freemasonry who have also been deceived. Note the deceptive practice used toward the Blue Degrees from one of Masonry's highest authoritative documents: In *Morals & Dogma*, Albert Pike wrote this for the superior degrees:

"The Blue Degrees are but the outer court or portico of the Temple. Part of the symbols are displayed there to the Initiate, but he is intentionally misled by false interpretations."

Accepting the Lordship of Jesus Christ over my life as I do, my Christian standing does not permit alliances with such pagan and deceitful practices.

Mackey gives attention to the issue of resignation or "demit" from the Lodge:

> The application for a demit is a matter of form, and there is no power in any Lodge to insist on any brother continuing a connection with it which he desires to sever.
>
> I proudly present this day _____ my notice of withdrawal in compliance with God's Word (2 Corinthians 6:14–18; Matthew 5:34–37; James 5:12; Galatians 1:8).
>
> Again I feel no animosity toward you, only toward the institution, which has, deceived us both.
>
> Respectfully yours,

GLOSSARY OF
MASONIC TERMS

Many Masonic expressions convey the idea of eternal benefits for Lodge members. Such implications only enhance the mythical overtones of righteousness before God, such as Masonry's "freedom from sin" or "spiritual temple." It would be impossible to define all the terms and symbols related to Freemasonry in only a few short pages; these are terms that are most pertinent to the subject matter of this book.

Most of these definitions are drawn from information contained in the *Encyclopedia of Freemasonry* (Mackey, McClenachan). Other resources are noted as well and all are cited in the Bibliography.

> **A.A.O.N.M.S.** – The abbreviation for Ancient Arabic Order, Nobles of the Mystic Shrine. Commonly known as the "Shriners," this is a social group of Freemasons who are either Knights Templar or 32nd-degree Scottish Rite Masons. Shriners, who were organized in New York City in 1872 and became a national body in 1876, are widely known for their support of hospitals for crippled children.

> **Acacia** – The acacia, referred to as "shittim" in the Bible, is a hardwood tree similar to the mulberry tree. In Freemasonry the acacia (or a sprig of cedar, in its place) is used to represent the immortality of the soul and further symbolizes innocence, implying freedom from sin. Freemasons wear evergreens at the funerals of their brethren and cast them into the grave.

> **Acacian** – One, who, by obedience, etc., is free from sin.

All-Seeing Eye – An ancient symbol of the Supreme Being used by the Freemasons. The ancient Egyptian god Osiris is said to be the All-Seeing Eye in the Lodges (see *Morals & Dogma,* pgs. 476, 477).

Altar – The holiest site in a Lodge, where candidates carry out rituals for membership. (See Chapter Three — Jeremiah 1:16: "And I will utter my judgments against them touching all their wickedness, who have forsaken me, and have burned incense unto other gods, and worshipped the works of their own hands.")

Apron – A distinctive piece of attire Masons wear to represent innocence in conduct and purity of heart.

Boaz – See Kabbala in Appendix A.

Broken Column – An emblem of Blue Masonry (first three degrees) that includes an image of a woman holding an evergreen branch and weeping over a broken column. Behind her, "time" stands combing her hair. The image is based on an Egyptian myth about goddess Isis (*Morals and Dogma,* pg. 379). (See Chapter Five.) Ezekiel 8:12-18 says the women were weeping for Tammuz (Osiris, Baal, Nimrod), where they worshipped the sun toward the East.

Builder – A title referring to Masons, who are said to be builders of a spiritual temple. Lodge teaching denies that Jesus is Lord and God's only begotten Son. So was Masonic influence what Jesus and Peter meant when they spoke of the "builders"? Yes (see "Stone, Rejected"): "The stone [Jesus, which the builders rejected, the same] is become the head of the corner (Mark 12:10; Luke 20:17; Acts 4:11,12).

Craft – A Masonic term defining the skill and practice of the art of Masonry itself while signifying the whole body of Freemasonry wherever it may be found.

Degrees – A signification describing the steps taken in Masonry by which one climbs up the rungs of the Order.

Dotage – A practice that forbids Lodge membership to certain older men who may possess the inability to keep the secrets of Masonry. This is contrary to the teaching of Christ, who said "whosoever" desires to come to Him can, for all things are open and do not need to be concealed.

Five-Pointed Star – Some researchers question whether this star, not to be confused with the blazing star, is indeed a Masonic emblem at all. At any rate, the five-pointed star, a noted symbol in Western magic, is said to symbolize spiritual aspirations when pointing up and bestiality and other dark behaviors when facing down. The inverted five-pointed star (one point downward) is the symbol of the Eastern Star branch of adoptive Masonry for the mothers, wives, sisters and daughters of Masons.

"G" – This letter, a familiar Mason symbol, represents the initial of God and is found in the Lodge above the Master's chair. It also represents "geometry" and "generative power."

Jacin – See Kabbala in Appendix A.

Jacob's Ladder – A symbol taken from Genesis 28 of the Bible and used to represent the "degrees," or steps, of the Masonic ladder that leads, ultimately, to spiritual enlightenment.

Jehovah – A name for God that means "self-existent" or "eternal" (Exodus 6:3). "It is speculated that operative

Masons of the Middle-Ages knew the indescribable name of God, although with much debate" (*Encyclopedia of Freemasonry*, pg. 363). The important thing is that Jesus or *Iesous* (Greek), which comes from the Hebrew name *Yehowshuwa*, means "Jehovah is salvation." This reflects that the Word (God) became flesh (Jesus) to seek and to save (John 1:14).

Jesus – Interestingly, *Encyclopedia of Freemasonry* lists many philosophers, reformers, so-called redeemers, false gods and theories but includes no heading for "Jesus," the only Redeemer. Only listed are headings like "Order of Christ."

Kabbala – See Appendix A.

Key – An important symbol of Masonry taken from the myths of the ancient Greek goddess Isis. Regarded as a symbol of secrecy in the Royal Arch Degree.

Mackey, Albert – 33rd-degree Mason (1807–1881) – A physician from Charleston, South Carolina considered by many to be America's most outstanding Masonic historian of his day. His books are used as references even today.

Magic – The art of capturing the secret powers of nature for self-gratification. White magic is used for beneficial purposes, while black magic is intended for harm. "It is certain that 'onomatology,' or the science of names, forms a very interesting part of the investigations of the higher Masonry, and it is only in this way that any connection can be created between the two sciences. Much light, it must be confessed, is thrown on many of the mystical names in the higher degrees by the dogmas of magic; and hence magic furnishes a curious and interesting study for the Freemason."

Obelisk – Monuments that were common in ancient Egypt, where they were erected to honor the sun god. Interestingly, the Washington Monument is an obelisk; George Washington is revered as a famous Mason.

Phallic Worship – An ancient practice that formed the origin of the "point within a circle."

Pillars of the Porch – See Appendix A.

Pike, Albert – 33rd-degree Mason – (1809–1891) – Famous Boston-born Scottish Rite Mason who was a teacher, a lawyer and a general in the Confederate Army. He earned respect while serving as a Grand Commander of the AASR (Ancient Accepted Scottish Rite) (Southern Jurisdiction) and remains famous for reviving the Scottish Rite and compiling the book, *Morals and Dogma*.

Point Within a Circle – A symbol used in Freemasonry in which the point represents a Mason and the circle a boundary line of his duty to God and man. Two perpendicular lines represent St. John the Baptist and St. John the Evangelist, the patron saints of the Order. The ancient roots of this symbol are tied to phallus worship practices and fecundity. The point within a circle is also said to represent the Lodge, its Master and Wardens.

Rains – A customary warning used among English Masons of the middle of the last century to announce the appearance of a profane; someone who is not initiated into Masonic rites. To be profane is to be irreverent to God or His principles. Masonry teaches that even ministers of the Gospel who are not members of the Lodge fit the category of "profane."

Rising Sun – A symbol of the Master of the Lodge.

Rose – Masons use the rose as a symbol of secrecy

(derived from the story of Venus) and immortality. The "rose of Venus" is found on the crosses in many churches.

Saints John the Baptist and John the Evangelist – The "patron saints" of Masonry.

Scottish Rite – Established in 1801 and consisting of 33 degrees, which are divided into seven sections:

1) Symbolic Lodge (first three degrees)
2) Lodge of Perfection (degrees four through 14)
3) Council of Princes of Jerusalem (degrees 15 and 16)
4) Chapter of Rose Croix (degrees 17 and 18)
5) Council of Kadosh (degrees 19 through 30)
6) Consistory of Sublime Princes of the Royal Secret (degrees 31 and 32)
7) Supreme Council (Degree 33)

Setting Sun – Represents the Senior Warden in the Lodge because of his duty to pay and dismiss the Craft at the day's end.

Shriners – See A.A.O.N.M.S.

Square and Compass – Symbolizes the Mason's duty and his brotherhood with others in the Lodge. Note that the compass is an instrument used to make the point within a circle. A square and compass is laid on top of the Bible or holy book in Lodges. This represents the superior stance given to these tools over God's Word, signifying good works above simple faith.

Star, Eastern – A part of "Adoptive Masonry" for the mothers, wives, sisters and daughters of Masons.

Stone – In Freemasonry, the unhewn stone is a symbol of man's evil and corrupt condition, while the smooth stone represented evil; Jehovah instructed an altar to be built of rough ones (see Exodus 20:25; Deuteronomy

27:6; Joshua 8:31).

Stone, Rejected – While Christians recognize this expression taken from Matthew 21:24 as Christ's reference to Himself, the Freemasons use it to convey the concept that a stone passed over just might turn out to be the most suitable one in a construction. That context belies the Mason doctrine's rejection of Christ as Lord.

Unity of God – The Freemason doctrine of universality; the organization recognizes and accepts so-called redeemers of all religions and deems them part of God or a component of the Godhead. It's important to remember, however, that the Godhead is not a conglomeration of different redeemers; it is triune—three-in-one — comprised of the Father, Son and the Holy Ghost (1 John 5:7).

Widow's Son – A title used in ancient Masonry to refer to Hiram, the architect of [Solomon's] Temple. Today this term is included as an aid to escape the judgment of a crime committed by a Mason. For example, if a Mason is brought before a criminal court on a charge, and he cries, "Is there no help for a Widow's Son?" Masons who may be either judge or juror are obligated to help their brother Mason evade judgment.

York Rite – The oldest of all the Rites, which originally included only three degrees:

1) Entered Apprentice; 2) Fellow-Craft; 3) Master Mason.

BIBLIOGRAPHY

1) *The Holy Bible*

2) Albert Pike, *Morals and Dogma* (Washington, D.C.: The Roberts Publishing Company, 1950).

3) H.B.V. Voorhis, *Facts for Freemasons* (Richmond, VA: Macoy Publishing and Masonic Supply Co., Inc., 1951,1979).

4) E. F. Elson & Alberta Peck, *The Art of Speaking* (Boston, MA: Ginn and Company, 1966).

5) Merrill F. Unger, *Unger's Bible Dictionary* (Chicago, Ill.: Moody Bible Institute, 1957, 1961, 1966).

6) Henry H. Halley, *Halley's Bible Handbook* (Grand Rapids, MI: Zondervan Publishing House, 1927, 1928, 1929, 1931, 1932, 1933, 1933, 1934, 1936, 1938, 1939, 1941, 1943, 1944, 1946, 1948, 1951, 1955, 1957, 1959, 1962, 1965).

7) Walter Lewis Wilson, *Wilson's Dictionary of Bible Types* (Grand Rapids, MI: Eerdmans Printing Co., 1957).

8) Alexander Hislop, *The Two Babylons* (In America: Loizeaux Brothers, Inc.; In England: A&C Black, LTD., 1916, 1943, 1959).

9) A. E. Waite, *The Holy Kabbala* (New York, The MacMillan Company) 1929; (London and Tonbridge, The Whitfriars Press) 1929.

10) Dr. William Smith, *Smith's Bible Dictionary* (Nashville, TN: Holman Bible Publishers)- no date.

11) Tyndale House Publishing, *New Bible Dictionary* (The Inter-Varsity Fellowship) 1962.

12) Nevill Drury, *Dictionary of Mysticism and the Occult* (San Francisco, Cambridge, Hagerstown,

New York, Philadelphia, London, Mexico City, Sao Paulo, Singapore, Sydney: Harper & Row, Publishers,) 1985.

13) David Leeming, *Mythology* (Verona, Italy: Europa Verlag, Mondadori:)1976.

14) Evelyn Rossiter, *The Book of the Dead* (Printed in Spain: Crown Publishers, Inc., British Museum).

15) Ken Wolf, *Personalities and Problems* (Lexington, MA: Ginn Press) 1985.

16) Albert Mackey 33rd-degree and Charles T. McClenachan 33rd-degree, *Encyclopedia of Freemasonry* (Chicago, New York, London: The Masonic History Company) 1921.

17) Grand Lodge of Illinois, *What is Freemasonry?* (Issued by the Grand Lodge of Illinois, A.F. & A.M. Committee on Masonic Information) 1949,1965.

18) James Strong, *Strong's Exhaustive Concordance of the Bible Hebrew and Greek Reference* (World Bible Publishing) 1992.

19) Tom McKenney, *The Good Word,* www.wordsfor living.org.

20) Grand Lodge of Illinois, *Freemasonry's Attitude Toward Politics and Religion,* (Issued by the Grand Lodge of Illinois, A.F. & A.M., Committee on Masonic Information) 1949.

21) Emmanuel Rebold and J. F. Brennan *The Stand(ard) History of Freemasonry,* (Cincinnati, OH: J.F. Frennan) 1885.

22) Edmond Romayne, *Handbook of Freemasonry* (P.R.C. Publications, Inc) 1943 (Chicago, Ill.:

Charles T. Powner Co) 1973.

23) Albert Mackey 33rd-degree, *Masonic Ritualist, Mackey's Masonic Ritualist: Monitorial Instructions in the Degrees from Entered Apprentice to Select Master* (Clark & Maynard Publishers: New York) 1867.

24) General Welsh, *Freemasonry on Trial.*

25) Capt. WM. Morgan, *Illustrations of Masonry* (Chicago, Illinois: Ezra A. Cook Publications, Inc.) 1827,1982, 1926, 1982.

26) Manly P. Hall, *Initiates of The Flame* (Los Angeles, CA: The Phoenix Press) 1934.

27) Manly P. Hall, *The Lost Keys of Freemasonry,* (Richmond, VA: Hall Publishing Company)1924.

INDEX

A

Abram, 57
Abraham, spiritual house of, 58
Acacia, 65, 154
Acacian, 154
Adam, Kabbala passed to, 130
Adonay, 78
Adoptive Masonry, 97
Ahura Mazda, 131
Allah, 87,89,92
All-Seeing Eye, 69,155
Altar, 155
Antichrist, 22,142
Ancient Arabic Order, Nobles of the Mystic Shrine, 87,154
Ancient Mysteries, 62,137,139
Apis, 71,73
Apollo, spirit of, 151
Apprentice Degree, 39,47
Apron, 31,155
Ashtaroth, 144

B

Baal, 11,41,61,69,70,89,125,142
Baalim, 21,107,142
Baphomet, 76,77,82,102
Baptism, 17,127
Bel, 62,89,143,145
Bible, furniture of the Lodge, 16,17,32,33,38
Bible, kissing of, 42,50
Blue Degrees, 23,47,67,119,122,152
Boaz, 132,155
Body, severed, 47,52
Bowels, burned to ashes, 47,52
Breast, torn open, 50
Brigham Young, 79

Broken Column, 155
Brotherhood Religion, 43,44
Buddha, first Masonic legislator, 133
Builder, 155
Bull, as Apis, 72,73

C

Calf, 71,72
Chaldeans, 100
Chaos, 143
Chastity, 51
Chemosh, 61
Child Sacrifice, 125
Christ, office of, 20
Christian Impact, 112
Christianity, origin different from Masonry, 24
Church, governing positions, 16,76,81,110,113
Confusion of languages, 59,63,142,145
Confucius, 21,23
Craft, 49,58,156
Creation, 10 emanations of, 131
Crescent Moon, 92
Cush, 142,145

D

Deception, 23,27,40,80,98
Degrees, 156
DeMolay, Order of, 103
Devil, raising the, 82
Diana, 144
Discrimination, 110
Distress, grand hailing sign of, 51
Dotage, 51,156

E

Eastern Star, 96,98,101,156
Eastern Star, five degrees of, 97
Eastern Star, motto of, 99
Egypt, 11,57,62,64,70
Egyptian Bondage, 71
Egyptian Legend 11,70,120,130

F

False Masonry, 136
False Prophet, 142
Familiar Spirit, 100,149
Fellowship, five points of, 66
Fez, 91
Five-Pointed Star, 101,156
Free, definition of, 11
Freemasonry and the New Age, 102,148,149
Freemasonry, good works of, 16,30,90,110,159
Freemasonry, preceded Christianity, 56
Freemasonry, root of the Eastern Star, 103
Freemasonry, spirit of, 81

G

"G", 156
Gabriel, 86
Generational curse, 96
Gnostics, 99
Goat, riding the, 82
Goat, uses of, 82
God, above all the Baalim, 21,107
God, belief in, 18
God, general names for, 19

God, manifest in the flesh, 81
Godhead, 27,134,160
Goddesses, origin of, 142
Good Works, 16,30
Grand Lodge Practice, 20
Grand Lodge for Blacks, 108
Grand Warden of Heaven, 19
Great Architect of the Universe, 19

H

Ham, 57
Hermaphrodite, 51
High Places, 41
Hiram, 25,57,64,67
Hiram Abiff, legend of, 64
Horoscopes, 148
Huram, 67
Husband of the Mother, 144

I

Idolatry, 73,146
Idols, kissing of, 42
Imperialism, 143
Isis, as moon, 68,120,144
Islam, born from military conquest, 91
Islam, five pillars of, 86
Islam, form of Baal worship, 89
Israel, ten tribes of, 73

J

Jacin, 156
Jacob's Ladder, 156
Japheth, 57
Jehovah, 22,79,156
Jesus, no listing of, 157

Jesus, as reformer, 34,38
Jesus, is God, 80
Jesus, not crucified for the sin of the world, 86
Jesus, not permitted to pray in the name of, 20
Jesus, freedom from bondage, 104
Job's Daughters, 103
Joseph Smith, 79
Jubela, 65
Jubelo, 65
Jubelum, 65

K
Kabbala, 119,130,155,157
Kabbala, a Jewish mystical philosophy, 133
Kabbala, communicated to angels, 130
Key, 157
Khir-Om Abi, 68
Koran, 87
Krishna, 148
Ku Klux Klan, 108, 109

L
Languages, confusion of, 59,61,142
Legislator, 19,133
Light, 11,39
Light, biblical use of, 38,40,44
Light, false, 43
Light, sons of, 38,40
Lights, great, 32
Lion's Paw Grip, 25,66
Lodge, Boasts of, 10,19,56

Lodge, Celestial, 31,110
Lodge deception, 23,27,40,80,98
Lodge, irregular or clandestine, 51,107,136
Lodge, membership in decline, 113
Lodge Morality, 10,16,23,77,121
Lodge, secrets protected, 10,46,48,52,97,122
Lodge, temple of religion, 18
Lowest Valleys, 41
Lucifer, as god of Masonry, 77
Lucifer, is God, 77,78
Lucifer, light-bearer, 79

M
Mackey, Albert, 157
Magi, 99
Magic, 100,102,132,157
Magic, curious study for Masons, 99
Mah-Hah-Bone, 66
Masonic Science, 131
Masonry, identical with mystery religions 76,119,139
Masonry, reverences all great reformers, 23
Merodach, 61,69,142
Mohammed, 23,32,86,91,121
Moloch, 61,145
Moody, D.L., 88,126
Mormon Brotherhood, 79
Moses, 23,71,119
Mother and Child, 144
Murder, 52,67,145
Muslim, 18,86,91

Mutilation, penalty of, 40
Mysteries, birthplace of, 62
Mysticism, Eastern, 148

N

New Age, 148
Negro Lodges, 108
New World Order, 121
Nimrod, 59,60,70,77,142
Nimrod, Baal synonymous, 71
Noachidae, 58
Noah, father and founder, 58
Noah, flood of, 59,137

O

Oath, Apprentice Degree, 47
Oath, Second Degree, 49
Oath, Third Degree, 50
Obelisk, 64,158
Old Man in Dotage, 51,156
Operative Masonry 11,156
Order, binding of, 54
Osiris, 57,64,68,120,144
Osiris, compared to Hiram, 67
Osiris, everything good in nature comes from, 68
Osiris, identical to Baal, 63
Out-of-body experiences, 148
Oxen, cutting of, 146

P

Paganism, 72,76,80,96,109
Paganism, curse of, 96
Pastors, destroyed vineyards, 41
Paul, 119
Pentagram, 102
Phallus, 64,72,158

Phallic Worship, 158
Philosophy, 24,27
Philosophy, a kind of journey, 25
Philosophy, Masonic history is the, 11
Philosophy of regeneration, 26
Pike, Albert, 158
Pillars of the Porch, 158
Point Within a Circle, 158
Prayer, 19,21,107,115
Priesthood, ancient, 63
Prince Hall Lodges, 108
Pythagoras, 120
Python, 150

R

Racism, 108
Rainbow Girls, 103
Rains, 158
Raised, 25
Ramadan, 86
Religion, 17,89
Resurrection, 24,43,66,68
Reversal of Roles, 79,107,146
Rising Sun, 158
Roman Road, 126
Rose, 158

S

Saints John the Baptist and John the Evangelist, 39,159
Satan, 43,73,76,81,142
Satanism, 148
Scottish Rite, 154,158,159
Secrets, Master Mason's, 10,52
Sectarian Character, 19
Semiramis, 77,142,145

Setting Sun, 159
Shem, 57,145
Shemites, 57
Shinar, 59,70
Shrine Club, 87
Shrine Club, party animals of Freemasonry, 90
Shrine Club, supports Islam, 88
Shrine, for Diana, 144
Shrine Hospitals, 89
Shrine, red hat, 91
Shriners, all are Masons, 87
Sodomy, 125
Solomon, 11,25,32,65
Solomon, did evil in the sight of the Lord, 71
Solomon, legend conjured, 70
Solomon's Temple, 65
Speculative Masonry, 137
Spirit of Divination, 150
Spiritual Bondage, 81,96,103,110
Spurious Masonry, 136
Square and Compass, 32,159
Star, Five-pointed, 156
Star, Eastern, 159
Star out of Jacob, 100
Stone, Rejected, 155,160
Strong Grip, 25,66
Sun, worship of, 62
Superiority of Freemasonry, 103,106
Sword, key of heaven and hell, 91

T
Talisman, 131,133
Tammuz, 61,155

Tara Center, 149
Tarot, 132
Temples, 17
Third Degree Ritual, 65
Thomas Jefferson 12
Throat, cut across, 47,48
Tower of Babel, 61,63,70,76,142
Tree of Life, Kabbalistic, 132
Trinity of Baalim, 142,145
Typhon, believed to be Shem, 145

U
Unity of God, 160
Universality, 19,56,133

W
Widow's Son, 160
Wise Men, 99
Witchcraft, 82,99,102,148
Wizards, 149
World, of one language, 61
Worshipful Lodge, 106
Worshipful Master, 42,66,69

Y
York Rite, 160

Z
Zoroaster, 21,23,131

MORE BOOKS BY KEITH HARRIS

The Unveiling

The Unveiling is a verse by verse study of the book of Revelation. The book of Revelation is greater than any mystery novel or suspense thriller. *The Unveiling* supplies answers to many perplexing questions of life: What happens after death? Is the earth going to be our eternal dwelling? Who will be at the Great White Throne Judgment? What comes after the Millennium? *The Unveiling* probes areas of Revelation not normally ventured by today's theologians, making it a most enlightening and adventurous journey pertaining to life and the complexities of the afterlife. Fully outlined, indexed, cross-referenced and charted for easy access to any given aspect of Revelation.
490 pages -$16.99

When Death Comes

If you have ever been called upon to counsel the aged, the terminally ill, or those who are just beginning to question the mysteries of life and death, you will realize that mere human perspective is not enough to satisfy the mind. Personal opinions, near-death experiences, out-of-body phenomena, or fantastic dream-world ideas cannot supply the proper and satisfactory answers to our questions. *When Death Comes* is a biblically based study answering life's questions about death and what occurs thereafter. This study is a great tool for the minister as well as the layman who wishes to have answers to some of life's most puzzling questions. What about suicide? The death of a child? Heaven? Hell? Burial vs. cremation? All of these issues and more are addressed in this book.
224 pages - $12.99

The Bridal Feast

Have you ever wanted a complete study on the Lord's Supper? Have you wondered why the gospels record the event differently? Should the bread used in Communion service be leavened or unleavened? Is there a right or wrong use of the bread? What wine should Christians use in the Communion service, fermented or nonfermented? When Jesus turned water into wine, was it fermented wine or grape juice? This book answers these questions and many more. Find the explanation to the false teaching of transubstantiation. Put to rest the argument of moderate alcohol consumption. Fully indexed for quick reference to comments and Scriptures.
151 pages - $10.00

The Jurassic Mark: The Mystery of the Lost World

Here's a facinating book concerning the age-old mystery of the dinosaurs. Many Christians have been tripped up over this subject, falling victim to the illogical and fallacious arguments of humanist scientists. This book will answer questions on these and other topics: The Big Bang; Evolution; Carbon-14 Testing; Missing Links; The Two Floods of Scripture; Scriptural Gaps; Science and Christianity; The "Why" of Dinosaur Existence, and many other aspects relevant to understanding the dinosaur puzzle.
203 pages - $10.00

You may purchase these books from:
Omega Publishing, P.O. Box 1353, Madisonville, KY 42431
or
scripture2scripture.com
or
Midnight Call Ministries
POB 280008, Columbia, SC 29228